'A Moment White'

by
John Cairney

Research Material
by
Alannah O'Sullivan

Illustration and Typography
by
Irene Dickson

Photography of Press Cuttings
by
Bob Fleming

Original Idea
by
Roy McCallum

JOHN CAIRNEY has been associated with Robert Burns for more than twenty years of his professional life as an actor and writer. From his beginning with 'THERE WAS A MAN' at the Traverse Theatre in 1965, through various Edinburgh festivals, and tours around the world with 'THE ROBERT BURNS STORY', his one-man portrayal of the poet has been seen in nearly every country in the world and several times on television.

He has also written a six-part television serial based on the life, which was shown on Scottish television, and has made a long playing record and cassette on the same subject for R.E.L. Records, Edinburgh.

He founded the award-winning Burns festival in Ayr during 1976 with the assistance of the Kyle and Carrick District Council and the Scottish Tourist Board, and wrote several special dramatic pieces on the Burns theme for subsequent festival performance.

He considers the ultimate Burns statement will be to stage a full-scale Burns musical and see the Robert Burns story as an international feature film.

Price: Five Pounds

INTRODUCTION

On 31 July, 1786, six hundred and eighteen copies of a small book were printed at Kilmarnock under the title, *Poems, Chiefly in the Scottish Dialect* by Robert Burns. It sold out within a week, and a second edition came out the following year in Edinburgh. And so Robert Burns emerged from Ayrshire and went round the world to become the international figure he now is. Roy McCallum, the Creative Director of a Scottish Advertising Agency (and an Ayrshireman), felt that the time was right to display the works of Robert Burns alongside 200 years of history.

The idea behind this publication is that Robert Burns has a continuing appositeness and relevance to the human condition today as much as he had two hundred years ago. It was felt that a look at his work against the parade of the two hundred years since he first set down his lines would throw an interesting light, not only on what he wrote, but on those he wrote about. He was a keen and witty observer of man in his social scene, and the combination of his poetic perceptions and the hard news provided by the facts used in illustration might allow the reader an amusing and interesting comparison.

Approach was made to Arnold Kemp, Editor of the Glasgow Herald, for his co-operation. The newspaper had had its own bi-centenary in 1983. Its story was the story of Burns' day till our own, and from its files we might see how far or how little we had come. Marketing Manager, Derek Gilhooley, undertook to see the project through, and authority was given to Alannah O'Sullivan to research the Herald records. With the help of Mr Fisher and his excellent staff at the Mitchell Library, she selected appropriate items on micro-film, which were then photographed by Mr Bob Fleming for reproduction in the following pages.

I have added my own commentary to each of the twenty decades, as it occurred to me in reading the different stories, and have appended a Burns extract, either a poem or song. After the long period I have been involved with him, either as a subject for study, or a recourse for pleasure and a character to play, I have felt emboldened to indicate what I consider Burns' attitude might have been. This is entirely a personal comment, less than an intention to confirm the already well-known facts. If what he says has lived all this time, it will survive whatever I say. We place his living words against the life that has gone on since he wrote them. To those who know him, Robert Burns is an endless celebration of everyday and a constant inspiration. He is now a tradition and a legend, but he was also once a man who lived in Scotland and read his newspaper!

Glasgow,
October 1986

John Cairney

GLASGOW ADVERTISER,
AND
EVENING INTELLIGENCER.

No. 475.]   From MONDAY, June 7.—to FRIDAY, June 11. 1790.   [Vol. VIII.

LONDON.

HIS MAJESTY'S BIRTH-DAY.

Yesterday being the King's Birth-day, when his Majesty entered the 53d year of his age, it was observed as a high festival. The Court at St. James's Palace was very numerous, and consisted, among others, of the following persons of distinction. Of the Royal Family, their Majesties, his Royal Highness the Prince of Wales, Princess Royal, Duke of York, Dukes of Gloucester and Cumberland, Princesses Augusta, Elizabeth, and for the first time, the Princess Sophia, the Duke of Gloucester's daughter; the Duke of Orleans, the French, Spanish, and Sardinian Ambassadors, Prussian, Dutch, Russian, Saxon, Hungarian, Bavarian, Neapolitan, Venetian, and other Envoys and Secretaries; the Countess de la Luzerne, Baroness Nolken, Baron Robeque, Monsieur Colonne, and a few other foreigners; the Lord Chancellor; Archbishops of Canterbury and York; Chancellor of the Exchequer; Master of the Rolls; Attorney and Solicitor General; Judges of the Court of King's Bench and Common Pleas; Lord Mayor of London; Bishops of London, Winchester, Salisbury, Oxford, Peterborough, Worcester, Chester, Lincoln, Gloucester, Carlisle, Bangor, St. David's, Exeter, Bristol, Elphin, &c. all the Officers of State; Marquis of Bath (Lord in Waiting); Lord Dover (Gold Stick); and a great number of Nobility of both sexes.

At half past five o'clock the Drawing-room broke up when their Majesties and the Princesses retired.

LADIES DRESSES.

THE QUEEN was dressed in all the splendour of Majesty, as is usual on the birth-day of the King. There was something finely picturesque in her dress, her petticoat being very beautifully embroidered in imitation of clouds with shades of green foil; the drapery drew up with green bands covered with chains of diamonds and pearls.— The bands were trimmed at the ends with bunches of oak, and large diamond stars in the middle. The drapery of the corners was tied up with large diamond and pearl bows and bunches of oak. The trimming of the bottom was a deep blond lace.

Her Majesty wore a profusion of diamonds both about her dress and in her hair, with a diamond necklace, ear-rings, and stomacher.

The Princess Royal.—A white crape petticoat with silver spangles. The drapery was most superbly embroidered, the upper part being richly spangled, the under part sprigged with white and silver. The two draperies were divided with a rich fringe of oak leaves, elegantly embroidered with bows. The bottom was fringed with tassels.

Princess Augusta and Elizabeth were both dressed exactly the same. Their dress were a rich white and silver embroidered crape, with green and silver spangles. Across the bottom were festoons of green leaves, drawn up at the corners with rich embroidered bows. The bottom was fringed with green purple and white tassels.

The head dresses of the Princesses were ornamented with ostrich feathers, and a profusion of diamonds.

Burns, like Wordsworth, Roscoe and Thomas Paine, had an unquenchable ideal of the brotherhood of man. The last's admirable, though inflammatory, pamphlet, 'The Rights of Man', was distributed illegally throughout Scotland by Thomas Muir of Huntershill, and for doing so, he was transported to Botany Bay. Yet Burns, who praised it openly in Dumfries, was untouched, only suffering several tense appearances before the Excise Board. It would seem he still had well-placed friends; and anyway he was more than capable of making his own comment:

> 'For thus the royal mandate ran,
> When first the human race began,
> The social, friendly, honest man—
> What'er he be,
> 'Tis he fulfils great Nature's plan,
> And none but he!

There could be no more definite assertion of the rights of the ordinary man in the face of Kings. Burns, himself, was less anti-monarchist than anti-Hanoverian. He could never hide his distaste for the 'wee German lairdie' and his dull queen, nor could he ever disguise his sympathies for the romantic and still attractive Jacobites:

> 'The injured Stewart line is gone,
> A race outlandish fills their throne,
> An idiot race to honour lost,
> Who know them best, despise them most.'

Is there, for honest Poverty
    That hings his head, and a' that;
The coward-slave, we pass him by,
    We dare be poor for a' that!
For a' that, and a' that,
    Our toils obscure, and a' that,
The rank is but the guinea's stamp,
    The Man's the gowd for a' that.—

What though on hamely fare we dine,
    Wear hoddin grey, and a' that.
Gie fools their silks, and knaves their wine,
    A Man's a Man for a' that.
For a' that, and a' that,
    Their tinsel show, and a' that,
The honest man, though e'er sae poor,
    Is king o' men for a' that.—

Ye see yon birkie ca'd, a lord,
    Wha struts, and stares, and a' that,
Though hundreds worship at his word,
    He's but a coof for a' that.
For a' that, and a' that,
    His ribband, star and a' that,
The man of independent mind,
    He looks and laughs at a' that.—

A prince can make a belted knight,
    A marquis, duke, and a' that,
But an honest man's aboon his might,
    Gude faith he mauna fa' that!
For a' that, and a' that,
    Their dignities, and a' that,
The pith o' Sense, and pride o' Worth,
    Are higher rank than a' that.—

Then let us pray that come it may,
    As come it will for a' that,
That Sense and Worth, o'er a' the earth
    Shall bear the gree, and a' that.
For a' that, and a' that,
    Its comin yet for a' that,
That Man to Man the warld o'er,
    Shall brothers be for a' that.—

He scratched these lines on the window of an inn during his Highland tour in 1787. Wisely, he kicked the pane out later! Not for nothing was his a healthy pragmatism. But people had noticed. His open sympathies for the American Revolution in 1777 and the French in 1789, coupled with his ongoing championship of the common man, did him no good in his final years. His wide circle of influential friends, who might have proved generous patrons, gradually narrowed till few indeed remained. He never ceased to speak out. In this respect, he was his own worst enemy. But what a friend to the ordinary people, to whom he was, and still is, a hero. He could never forget he was a peasant himself, albeit an extraordinary one, and he resented bitterly the servility his station often forced on him, especially towards those to whom he felt innately superior. He readily admitted his heart ran before his head, but he was often forced to let his head rule where his heart rebelled. After all, he had a family to keep. But the 'independent wish' had been well 'planted' in his mind, and he could never quite shake off his sense of the individual's worth, and the value of each and every man to himself and to his God. Burns' constant reading of the Bible might have reminded him of the old Hasidic prayer — 'Grant us, O Lord, that we may never forget: every man and woman is the son or daughter of a King.'

Glasgow Herald.

MONDAY, JANUARY 6, 1806.

FOR JAMAICA,

For Martha Brae and Montego Bay,

THE New Ship ELIZABETH, JAS. GALT, master, and

For Lucea and Green Island,

The New Ship JANE, ROB. WYLLIE, master, lying at Greenock, and ready to take on board Goods, and will sail with the Feburary Convoy from Cork.

For freight or passage apply to the master at Greenock, or here to

STIRLING, GORDON & CO.

Glasgow, 1st Jan. 1806.

For New-York,

SPRING SHIP

'Musing on the roaring ocean
Which divides my love and me.'

Despite the fact that he was born with his back to the Atlantic Ocean, Burns made very few references to the sea in his works or letters. Even though he twice made plans to emigrate to Jamaica, there is only record of his actually being on board a ship on two occasions; once during the 'Rosamonde' incident on the Solway, and again when he was given a lift in a fishing boat on his way to visit his Burness cousins in Montrose. Yet, with the irony that is woven throughout the thread of his brief life, it was a sailor, Richard Brown, who first had the idea that young Burns' verses were worth printing. And, during his later troubles with Jean and the Armours, it was to the same Captain Brown he wrote in nautical fashion:

'I found Jean — with her cargo well laid in, unfortunately moored, at the mercy of wind and tide; I have towed her into harbour, where she may lie snug till she unload . . .'

Two years before, the 'marriage' had been officially annulled, but now Burns was under threat of a writ for maintenance of Jean's twins. Gavin Hamilton, his landlord, encouraged him to sell his share at Mossgiel and emigrate to the Indies as a plantation man. Burns acquiesced and booked a passage under Captain Smith on the 'Nancy'. Meantime, he prepared to put some of his verses in a little book as his friend, Brown, had suggested.

Will ye go to the Indies, my Mary,
   And leave auld Scotia's shore;
Will ye go to the Indies, my Mary,
   Across th' Atlantic roar.

O sweet grows the lime and the orange
   And the apple on the pine;
But a' the charms o' the Indies
   Can never equal thine.

I hae sworn by the Heavens to my Mary,
   I hae sworn by the Heavens to be true;
And sae may the Heavens forget me,
   When I forget my vow!

O plight me your faith, my Mary,
   And plight me your lily-white hand;
O plight me your faith, my Mary,
   Before I leave Scotia's strand.

We hae plighted our truth, my Mary,
   In mutual affection to join:
And curst be the cause that shall part us,
   The hour, and the moment o' time!!!

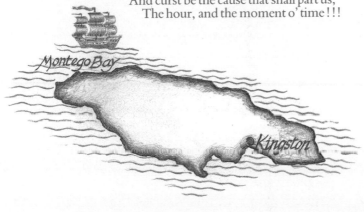

Around the same time, Burns admired a young girl in Tarbolton Kirk for the intensity with which she read her Bible. This was Mary Campbell, a highland-born, Gaelic-speaking nursery maid who had newly come to the district. Burns was intrigued by her appearance of piety, but it may have been only that she found difficulty in reading King James's English! With the help of a blackfoot, he made her acquaintance, and soon was in love again. On the second Sunday in May they met by arrangement where the Fail runs into the Doon, and solemnly exchanged Bibles over the running water — 'And ye shall not swear by my name falsely; I am the Lord.' (Leviticus 19:12). Willingly, Mary Campbell agreed to emigrate to the Indies with him. She was from a family of sailors and had no qualms about crossing the ocean. They planned to meet at the Port of Greenock once he had the book out. When it appeared, it sold in a week. Suddenly he was famous. He fixed a later sailing on the 'Roselle'. Mary waited. Friends advised a second edition in Edinburgh, and still Mary waited. Then one day he got a letter by the carter. Mary had died at Greenock from a fever. Burns was devastated — and guilt-stricken. He was never able to forget his enigmatic Mary Campbell. She has since passed into legend as his Highland Mary.

Glasgow Herald.

FRIDAY, NOVEMBER 3, 1815.

commenced the same match, viz. ⸺ ⸺ ⸺ in 21 days. He began on Monday morning.

A Sensible Pig.—A curious case occurred at the Union Hall Office on Saturday. A man who some time ago lost a pig, discovered it, a few days since, at the house of a widow lady in the neighbourhood. He applied for his property, but the lady refused to give it up, saying she had bought it. The man obtained the Magistrate's order for the attendance of both lady and pig at the office. The lady deposed as to the time when she purchased the pig. The man claiming it unfortunately could not swear to the day on which he lost it; but he requested that the Magistrate would order the pig to be turned loose in the street, and he would place a 10*l.* note on his back, and if the pig did not immediately go to his old stye, he would willingly forfeit both pig and note. The experiment was tried, and the pig was no sooner liberated, than, as the man had foreseen, he set off at full speed, and did not stop till he reached the yard of his original master.

It may only be coincidental that the poem in which Burns deals directly with an animal subject yields the longest title in his listed works! His genuine affection for the beast is obvious, despite his countryman's realistic attitude to animals generally. He saw them as fellow-creatures on earth and partners in the work of the farm. The only anthropomorphic extensions of his poetic fancy are with Luath and Caesar in 'The Twa Dugs', and to a lesser extent in 'The death and dying words of poor Maillie', a pet sheep. Life was too hard for both man and beast for anything less than a sharp awareness of the need to survive, especially in winter. Yet this was the season that Burns loved best. It gave him his only real leisure, and one can even now feel the white snow-stillness of the farm on New Year's morning as the old farmer gives a Ne'erday present to his horse. The genuine love of the animal shown here only underscores Burns' deep humanitarianism. In all his writing relating to horses, dogs, sheep and birds, he takes every advantage of his countryside experience and a life-time's observation to make his philosophical analogy and the social point. The conversation between 'The Twa Dugs' is a telling satire on the gap in station between the gentry and the peasantry. The comment in 'To A Louse' is moralistic. To see ourselves as others see us is no less expressed in being

The Auld Farmer's New-year-morning Salutation to his Auld Mare, Maggie, on giving her the accustomed ripp of corn to hansel in the New-year

Excerpt from

A *Guid New-year* I wish thee, Maggie!
Hae, there's a ripp to thy auld baggie:
Tho' thou 's howe-backet, now, an' knaggie,
     I've seen the day,
Thou could hae gaen like ony staggie
     Out-owre the lay.

Tho' now thou 's dowie, stiff an' crazy,
An' thy auld hide as white 's a daisie,
I've seen thee dappl't, sleek an' glaizie,
     A bonie gray:
He should be tight that daur't to *raize* thee,
     Ance in a day.

Thou ance was i' the foremost rank,
A *filly* buirdly, steeve an' swank,
An' set weel down a shapely shank,
     As e'er tread yird;
An' could hae flown out-owre a stank,
     Like onie bird.

It's now some nine-an'-twenty year,
Sin' thou was my *Guidfather's Meere*;
He gied me thee, o' tocher clear,
     An' fifty mark;
Tho' it was sma', 'twas *weel-won* gear,
     An' thou was stark.

When I first gaed to woo my *Jenny*,
Ye then was trottan wi' your Minnie:
Tho' ye was trickie, slee an' funnie,
     Ye ne'er was donsie;
But hamely, tawie, quiet an cannie,
     An' unco sonsie.

That *day,* ye pranc'd wi' muckle pride,
When ye bure hame my bonie *Bride*:
An' sweet an' gracefu' she did ride
     Wi' maiden air!
Kyle-Stewart I could bragged wide,
     For sic a *pair*.

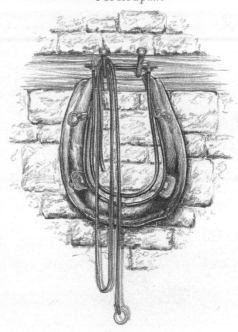

prompted by the examination of an insect on a young lady's bonnet as she sits in front of him in church. Her attractiveness is no hindrance to the point being made. He was as responsive to incongruity as he was to beauty. This was part of the wit of the man. And his charity could not be better illustrated than in his concern for that mouse in the harvest-field — a poor, 'wee cowerin', timorous beastie'. He knew well what it meant to be turned out of the house, and he shared a misgiving for the future, as great as anything the little mouse may have felt in being disturbed by Burns' plough. 'Thy wee bit hoosie too, in ruins . . .' His genius in these tender lines was that he could, like all great poets, take the particular situation, even as it related to the smallest animal, and make it reflect the larger situation of man in the world of nature. He knew we must relate to everything about us; the elements, the seasons, and all God's other creatures: 'A wee bird cam tae our ha' door . . .' Notice the frequent use of the diminutive! If Burns knew himself larger than the little mouse, he didn't feel himself superior. He recognised its animal nature as opposed to his human nature, but totally identified with the complete ecological sense of their living and surviving together in the same world.

Glasgow Herald.

MONDAY, APRIL 24, 1820.

The following is the petition of the Linlithgow-shire Farmers, submitted to the consideration of their brethren in Scotland:—

To the Hon. the House of Commons of Great Britain and Ireland, in Parliament assembled,

The humble Petition of the undersigned Occupiers of Land, and others interested in the state of Agriculture in the county of Linlithgow,

Sheweth,

That your petitioners are chiefly occupiers of land, which is appropriated to all sorts of grain, &c.

The enormous importation of foreign corn, has been such as to depreciate the price of grain, in general about sixteen shillings per quarter, below that which is a fair remuneration for the expenses necessarily and unavoidably incurred by the British farmer, who, from various causes, is unable to meet the foreign grower in the market upon equal terms.

That the present corn laws are altogether inadequate to prevent the evil complained of.

That your petitioners disclaim all intention of promoting their own interest at the expense of the rest of the community; but, considering, as they do, agriculture as the main spring of national prosperity, they feel convinced, that whilst it labours under its present depression, no other branch of industry can flourish.

That your petitioners have struggled for a length of time against difficulties which have threatened to overwhelm them, and are now driven to seek protection in the wisdom of Parliament, from that inevitable ruin which must eventually be their lot, along with the whole cultivators of the soil of the United Kingdom, unless prevented by some immediate, active, and salutary measure.

That your petitioners consider the permission of warehousing foreign corn duty free, and other productions of the soil nearly so, when the average prices are below the import price, to be the great cause of the evils complained of, and also the want of a fair general price being taken of Great Britain and Ireland, as the regulation for the corn laws.

Your petitioners beg leave to call the attention of your Honourable House to the great distress of the manufacturers throughout the kingdom, at a time when the importation of foreign corn never was known to be so great, by about one-half; consequently this is a flat contradiction to the idea, that our employing Foreign Agriculturists to raise corn for our use gives encouragement to our manufactories. The reverse, your petitioners think, must always be the case, as our country is drained of those millions of money, which would otherwise circulate amongst our home labourers, and, of course, would soon find its way to the manufacturers, shopkeepers, &c., all of whom are now starving for want of that employment which is now given to foreigners, owing to the deficient protection afforded to the British farmer.— Your petitioners therefore humbly solicit your Honourable House to take the same under your most serious consideration, and grant such relief as shall seem meet.

RWOOD.

Robert Burns died of his boyhood. At any rate, the endocarditis that killed him at thirty-seven stemmed from the rheumatic fever and colic that plagued him all his life. Both were rooted in the living and working conditions of his youth and early manhood on his father's various farms in Ayrshire. First at Mount Oliphant, then at Lochlea, and again at Mossgiel, he knew little more than the drab existence of the most miserable serf, working exhausted soil with meagre implements as long as there was light. Then to crawl home, too tired to eat his crowdie, too hungry to sleep in the damp straw. Helplessly, he had to watch his father battle against leases, the weather, the cost of improvements, the always-growing family, the greed of the landlords, the snarl of factors, until his body broke before his pride did. William Burnes took McLure, his landlord, to the High Court in Edinburgh on the matter of farm improvements, and won. But he got news of the victory on his deathbed and his son was left with a debt to the lawyers. 'Kind death' had snatched his father away, and Burns was left in charge of his brothers and sisters. But bad seed spoiled their first year, and a late harvest the next. Small wonder that Burns hated farming. His heart was never in it. His heart was in writing and reading and songs and convivial talk, not in crops and cattle, enclosures and fencing. But it was just as hard to make self-improvements as it was to make improvements on the land. Eventually, when he was able to better himself, he was still plagued by the twin curses of his volatile existence — barren soil and fertile women.

In his day, farming all over the country was at a low ebb and Ayrshire then was far from being the rich and prosperous county it is today. Not that Burns was a bad farmer. As a young man, he had won a prize for 'Lint Seed Saved for Sewing', and had gone to Irvine to learn flax-dressing — but even that investment went up in smoke in a Hogmanay fire! Even when he came to

Excerpt from

My father was a farmer upon the Carrick border O
And carefully he bred me, in decency and order O
He bade me act a manly part, though I had ne'er a farthing O
For without an honest manly heart, no man was worth regarding. O

Then out into the world my course I did determine. O
Tho' to be rich was not my wish, yet to be great was charming. O
My talents they were not the worst; not yet my education: O
Resolv'd was I, at least to try, to mend my situation. O

In many a way, and vain essay, I courted fortune's favor; O
Some cause unseen, still slept between, and frustrate each endeavour; O
Some time by foes I was o'erpower'd; sometimes by friends forsaken; O
And when my hope was at the top, I still was worst mistaken. O

Then sore harass'd, and tir'd at last, with fortune's vain delusion; O
I dropt my schemes, like idle dreams; and came to this conclusion; O
The past was bad, and the future hid, its good or ill untryed; O
But the present hour was in my pow'r, and so I would enjoy it, O

No help, nor hope, nor view had I; nor person to befriend me; O
So I must toil, and sweat and moil, and labor to sustain me, O
To plough and sow, to reap and mow, my father bred me early, O
For one, he said, to labor bred, was a match for fortune fairly, O

Thus all obscure, unknown, and poor, thro' life I'm doom'd to wander,
O
Till down my weary bones I lay in everlasting slumber; O
No view nor care, but shun whate'er might breed me pain or sorrow; O
I live today as well's I may, regardless of tomorrow, O.

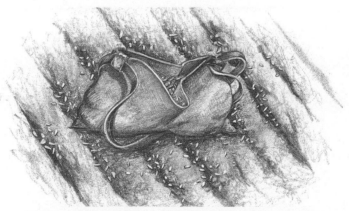

choose his own farm at Ellisland, near Dumfries in 1789, he did so more for its poetic views than for its commercial or agricultural potential. He might sentimentalise the farmer and his family in 'The Cotter's Saturday Night', or make a lively song of it in 'The Ploughman', but in his heart, he knew the stark, bitter pain of farming failure, and wanted nothing more to do with it. Nevertheless, it was at Ellisland in 1790, after marrying his Jean at last, he was to know the only truly happy year of his life. One afternoon, while walking near the farm, by the banks of the Nith, he was caught in a rainstorm, and sheltered under a tree. Jean came hurrying out with his coat to find him laughing. When he came home he started writing. Then, sitting on the table, by the light of the fire, and with a candle in his hand, he read to Jean and the terrified children and some of the working men what he had just written — 'The Tale of Tam o' Shanter'!

Glasgow Herald.

MONDAY, JUNE 9, 1834.

GENERAL ASSEMBLY.

SPEECH OF THE MODERATOR.

The following is the address of the Moderator to the Assembly at the close of its proceedings on Monday evening. After some observations on the important functions of the Assembly, legislative, judicial, and executive, he said:—'I trust the time will never arrive when the General Assemblies of our Church will sacrifice the independence or become the tools of any administration, or any party in the State, or abstain from the avowal of its sentiments on matters purely religious from the fear of giving offence to the civil authorities. But the time may come, and is perhaps not far distant, when our courage and steadfastness may be put to a severer trial than it has yet endured. From the present Administration we have nothing to fear—not only have we received from the Throne the renewed assurance of his Majesty's determination to maintain inviolate the rights and prerogatives of the Church of Scotland, but the leading members of the Administration have, in the most explicit manner, expressed a similar determination. One of them in particular, in his place in Parliament, has recently argued in favour of religious establishments, not on grounds of a temporary expediency, but on grounds immutable and perpetual, and of universal application. Yet it is impossible to deny that of late years very different and opposite opinions have been broached and maintained. Infidels, and men professing religion, and acting, not I hope in the spirit, but certainly on the principles of infidelity, have avowed their hostility to religious establishments of every form, and their purpose to wage a war of utter extermination against them. If, which may God in his mercy forbid! these pernicious opinions should gain the ascendency—if they should ever prevail in the British Senate and around the Throne of the Sovereign—and if, as the prelude to the overthrow of our Ecclesiastical Establishment, an infidel and anti-Christian Administration shall infringe the rights and privileges of the Church, and intermeddle with

'The cheerfu' supper done,
They round the ingle form a circle wide,
The sire turns o'er wi' patriarchal grace,
The big Ha'– bible, aince his father's pride.'

The picture Burns paints in 'The Cotter's Saturday Night' suggests a rural existence that was far from the truth he knew. But within it there were realities, and one of these was the family's deep commitment to the Bible and the Church in Scotland, as revealed in the Kirk Session. A commitment which Burns did not wholly share. The Kirk in his day was the centrepoint of the country people's existence. It not only laid down the rules for the Sabbath, but for the rest of the week as well, and parishes went in terror of the Elders' disapproval. As for the minister, he had a status only just under God's, and Daddy Auld, the minister at Mauchline, took every advantage of this proximity! He had long admired Burns' literary potential, but deplored his radical attitudes and sexual proclivities. Burns could reason with him, but found no grounds for discussion at all with the Session Elders, especially one, William Fisher, whose special subject was the uncovering of sins against the flesh within the Parish. Burns became his particular target. Fisher chose unwisely, because Burns answered with a satirical poem, distributed secretly around the district, which by the laughter it caused, loosened the hitherto tyrannical grip of the Kirk and its Elders, not only in Ayrshire, but all over Scotland. Precisely and with deadly effect, a man, an attitude, a whole age and a persistent Scottish tradition was captured in its entirety and nailed to the page. A generation of pseudo-piety and mock morality was made to look at itself through the eyes of one of its principal sinners, and the Kirk was never the same again! In Burns' eyes, the overriding sin was one of hypocrisy and sham:

'But I gae mad at their grimaces,
Their sighing, cantin', grace-proud faces,
Their three–mile prayers an' half-mile graces,
Their raxin' conscience,
Whase greed, revenge and pride disgraces
Waur nor their nonsense.'

In his allegorical 'Holy Fair', his 'Address to the Unco Guid', and various Epistles, he continued to pour scorn on the righteous, and make fun of the Holy Willies.

Holy Willie's Prayer

Excerpt from

O thou that in the heavens does dwell!
Wha, as it pleases best thysel,
Sends ane to heaven and ten to h--ll,
    A' for thy glory!
And no for ony gude or ill
    They've done before thee.—

I bless and praise thy matchless might,
When thousands thou has left in night,
That I am here before thy sight,
    For gifts and grace,
A burning and a shining light
To a' this place.—

What was I, or my generation,
That I should get such exaltation?
I, wha deserv'd most just damnation,
    For broken laws
Sax thousand years ere my creation,
    Thro' Adam's cause!

Yet I am here a chosen sample,
To shew thy grace is great and ample:
I'm here, a pillar o' thy temple
    Strong as a rock,
A guide, a ruler and example
    To a' thy flock.—

[O L--d thou kens what zeal I bear,
When drinkers drink, and swearers swear,
And singin' there, and dancin' here,
    Wi' great an' sma';
For I am keepet by thy fear,
    Free frae them a'.—]

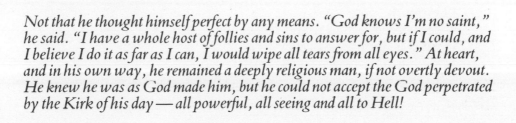

But yet—O L--d—confess I must—
At times I'm fash'd wi' fleshly lust;
And sometimes too, in wardly trust
    Vile Self gets in;
But thou remembers we are dust,
    Defil'd wi' sin.—

O L--d—yestreen—thou kens—wi' Meg—
Thy pardon I sincerely beg!
O may't ne'er be a living plague,
    To my dishonor!
And I'll ne'er lift a lawless leg
    Again upon her.—

Besides, I farther maun avow,
Wi' Leezie's lass, three times—I trow—
But L--d, that friday I was fou
    When I cam near her;
Or else, thou kens, thy servant true
    Wad never steer her.—

Maybe thou lets this fleshy thorn
Buffet thy servant e'en and morn,
Lest he o'er proud and high should turn,
    That he's sae gifted;
If sae, thy hand maun e'en be borne
    Untill thou lift it.—

L--d bless thy Chosen in this place,
For here thou has a chosen race:
But G--d, confound their stubborn face,
    And blast their name,
Wha bring thy rulers to disgrace
    And open shame.—

L--d hear my earnest cry and prayer
Against that Presbytry of Ayr!
Thy strong right hand, L--d make it bare
    Upon their heads!
L--d visit them, and dinna spare,
    For their misdeeds!

But L--d, remember me and mine
Wi' mercies temporal and divine!
That I for grace and gear may shine,
    Excell'd by nane!
And a' the glory shall be thine!
    Amen! Amen!

Not that he thought himself perfect by any means. "God knows I'm no saint," he said. "I have a whole host of follies and sins to answer for, but if I could, and I believe I do it as far as I can, I would wipe all tears from all eyes." At heart, and in his own way, he remained a deeply religious man, if not overtly devout. He knew he was as God made him, but he could not accept the God perpetrated by the Kirk of his day — all powerful, all seeing and all to Hell!

'Gie him strong drink until he wink
That's sinkin' in despair,
And liquor guid to fire his bluid,
That's pressed wi' grief and care.'

Penny ale was the plain man's opium. However poor, there still remained the need, at most, to dream and, at least, to forget. It was more than an opiate, it was also a release. In the conviviality and good cheer of the ale house or tavern, the poor man could forget his cares, and at the inn, the rich man enjoy his better fortune. The taste in Scotland was for French claret with all its latent Jacobite associations, as opposed to Spanish port or German hock, which were held to be the Hanoverian tipples. Contrary to received opinion, Burns was not a hard drinker. As he commented to Maria Riddell near the end of his life: "Madam, they would not thank me for my company if I did not drink with them. So I must give them all a slice of my constitution." And when Willie Nicol and Alan Masterton came to visit:

'Here are we met three merry boys,
Three merry boys, I trow, are we,
Mony a night we've merry been,
And mony mair we hope to be . . .'

It was thought he had swum through drink in his final Dumfries years. If so, how had he managed to write and arrange nearly four hundred songs? He

Scotch Drink

Let other Poets raise a fracas,
'Bout vines, an' wines, an' drunken *Bacchus*,
An' crabbed names an' stories wrack us,
   An' grate our lug,
I sing the juice *Scotch bear* can mak us,
   In glass or jug.

O thou, my Muse! guid, auld Scotch Drink!
Whether thro' wimplin worms thou jink,
Or, richly brown, ream owre the brink,
   In glorious faem,
Inspire me, till I *lisp* an' *wink*,
   To sing thy name!

Let husky Wheat the haughs adorn,
And Aits set up their awnie horn,
An' Pease an' Beans, at een or morn,
   Perfume the plain,
Leeze me on thee *John Barleycorn*,
   Thou king o' grain!

O *Whisky!* soul o' plays an' pranks!
Accept a *Bardie's* gratefu' thanks!
When wanting thee, what tuneless cranks
   Are my poor Verses!
Thou comes—they rattle i' their ranks
   At ither's arses!

Thee, *Ferintosh!* O sadly lost!
Scotland lament frae coast to coast!
Now colic-grips, an' barkin hoast,
   May kill us a';
For loyal *Forbes' Charter'd boast*
   Is taen awa!

Thae curst horse-leeches o' th' Excise,
Wha mak the *Whisky stills* their prize!
Haud up thy han' *Deil!* ance, twice, thrice!
   There, sieze the blinkers!
An' bake them up in brunstane pies
   For poor damn'd *Drinkers*.

Fortune, if thou'll but gie me still
Hale breeks, a scone, an' *Whisky gill*,
An' rowth o' rhyme to rave at will,
   Tak a' the rest,
An' deal't about as thy blind skill
   Directs thee best.

enjoyed a drink at the Globe tavern, where he had his special chair, and he had many haunts around the countryside. After all, he was a travelling man, an exciseman. He was also gregarious and popular. He liked company and talk and to entertain whenever the opportunity arose. Many a time on his late arrival at an inn, guests were wakened to be told that Poet Burns had arrived and one by one the guests would come in from their beds, eager to listen. As an exciseman, he made his own rules. In the regular search for illicit stills, he would arrive at the door of an old widow woman with his hat off, thus making it unofficial, to tell her that he would be back shortly with his hat on, which would make it official. She would then have time to make appropriate arrangements! He was as loved by the ordinary people in the countryside, as much as he was feared by the gentry. They might wince at his acerbic observations, but were quick to take advantage of his company at the table, and in their drunken games afterwards. At times, only his wit stood between him and social ridicule, for he knew full well that when 'guid drink gaes in, guid sense gaes oot'. This was the age of the five-bottle-a-night man, for whom drinking was a way of life, especially among the gentry and aristocracy. But as Findlater, his superior in the Excise noted, 'He was apt to prolong the social hour beyond the bounds which prudence would dictate, but in his family I will venture to say, that he was never otherwise than as attentive and affectionate to a high degree.'

The Glasgow Herald.

MONDAY MORNING, MARCH 6, 1848.

THE UNEMPLOYED.

In our fourth page will be found a notice of the proceedings of the unemployed on Friday. On Saturday a very large number of them again assembled on the Green, and in the afternoon processed in a strong body to the City Hall, in front of which they took up their position. Here the Relief Committee and the Magistrates were assembled, and received a deputation from the unemployed, who urged upon the authorities their destitute condition, and at the same time expressed their repugnance to accept employment at stone-breaking. Many of them followed in-door occupations, at which they desired to be employed, or failing this, in earth work, viz., delving and wheeling. The authorities represented their total inability to provide work of the kind required by the people; but after the deputation retired, a discussion ensued in a conversational tone, the result of which was a resolution to afford a gratuitous supply of meal the same evening —to open the soup kitchen on Monday (this day) for the temporary succour of the really destitute, and at the same time to endeavour to provide work, at least at stone-breaking, to as many as possible. The distribution of meal took place the same evening in the City Hall, in the presence of Bailies Stewart, Orr, R. Smith, D. Smith, and Gilmour; Mr. Hope, the Treasurer to the Relief Fund, Mr. Anderson, and other gentleman. The act of distribution was intrusted to a Committee of the unemployed themselves, and during the two or three hours it occupied, nothing like disorder or ill-feeling was exhibited; there being only the confusion inseparable from perhaps 2000 men and women contending with each other for precedence. Persons who were possessed of schedules, in proof that their cases had been inquired into by the Committee, and that they were really destitute, were supplied in the first instance, and afterwards all those who presented themselves were served without inquiry. This indiscriminate charity will not, we believe, be resorted to again. And there are good reasons why it should not. The remnant of the Relief Fund is already much reduced; and in the present state of the city it is difficult to see where or how it could be renewed. And again, were doles of this kind continued, the Committee would soon have 20,000 applicants on their hands. Stone-breaking, or out-of-door labour of any kind, must, we admit, be peculiarly severe in the case of men accustomed to light employment within doors; but, nevertheless, it is not easy to see how a somewhat hard labour-test can be dispensed with for the sake of the men themselves who are willing to work. On former occasions of public distress, the ranks of the unemployed have been invariably swelled by the rabble of the city—by men who are always idlers, even when employment is at a premium. Apply the labour-test to these persons, however, and they as invariably fall back on their own resources, and are heard of no more. Thus the honest workman is made to suffer from the imposture of those who claim to be his fellows, and will not work when they can get it. It will require, we are assured, no recommendation from us to induce the authorities to be as considerate with the deserving unemployed as the means at their disposal will admit.

'Some hae meat and canna eat,
Some hae meat that want it,
But we hae meat, and we can eat,
Sae let the Lord be thankit.'

In this grace, given extempore at a gentleman's table in Kirkcudbright, Burns was not only showing his ready and available wit, but also acknowledging that he was always grateful for anything he could get! He had been hungry enough as a boy to appreciate in later life the joys and rewards of the table. What is perhaps ironical is that the haggis, that most primitive of dishes, should be the food item so associated with him to this day. In his own day, it was like crowdie, extremely ordinary fare, and his address to it was done only in high-spirited mockery. He always realised that it was food like this that allowed him to survive the worst of the bad times, even though he was never really to enjoy total good health in his life.

Fair fa' your honest, sonsie face,
Great Chieftan o' the Pudding-race!
Aboon them a' ye tak your place,
      Painch, tripe or thairm:
Weel are ye wordy of a *grace*
      As lang 's my arm.

The groanin trencher there ye fill,
Your hurdies like a distant hill,
Your *pin* wad help to mend a mill
      In time o' need,
While thro' your pores the dews distil
      Like amber bead.

His knife see Rustic-labour dight,
An' cut you up wi' ready slight,
Trenching your gushing entrails bright
      Like onie ditch;
And then, O what a glorious sight,
      Warm-reekin, rich!

Then, horn for horn they stretch an' strive,
Deil tak the hindmost, on they drive,
Till a' their weel-swall'd kytes belyve
      Are bent like drums;
Then auld Guidman, maist like to rive,
      Bethankit hums.

Is there that owre his French *ragout*,
Or *olio* that wad staw a sow,
Or *fricassee* wad mak her spew
      Wi' perfect sconner,
Looks down wi' sneering, scornfu' view
      On sic a dinner?

Poor devil! see him owre his trash,
As feckless as a wither'd rash,
His spindle shank a guid whip-lash,
      His nieve a nit;
Thro' bluidy flood or field to dash,
O how unfit!

But mark the Rustic, *haggis-fed*,
The trembling earth resounds his tread,
Clap in his walie nieve a blade,
      He'll mak it whissle;
An' legs, an' arms, an' heads will sned,
      Like taps o' thrissle.

Ye Pow'rs wha mak mankind your care,
And dish them out their bill o' fare,
Auld Scotland wants nae skinking ware
      That jaups in luggies;
But, if ye wish her gratefu' pray'r,
      Gie her a *Haggis*!

'I count my health the greatest wealth,
Sae long as I enjoy it.
I'll fear nae scant, I'll bode nae want,
As lang's I get employment.'

He always had to work for a living. Whether it was as ploughboy, farmer, exciseman, or poet, he knew he had to earn his daily bread, since no one was going to give him anything for nothing. This accounts for his long held abhorrence of inherited wealth and landed estates — his detestation of all the snobbish assumptions of the lesser gentry. They had no need to work, and could give their lives to play. If he didn't work, he didn't eat — nor did his family. And if you didn't eat, you died, and that's all there was to it! Naturally, he would have preferred to have earned his living solely as a writer. He had the talent, the industry, the application, the temperament for the literary life, but he was never able to secure the opportunity. There had been talk of his taking the chair of Rhetoric at Edinburgh University and even that of Agriculture, but these sinecures came to nothing. Neither did a mooted appointment to the Salt Office at Dumfries, which only resulted in his being hired as a common guager. He had to take it. He had to eat. As he said, "the question is not what door of Fortune's palace we will enter by, but which she will open to us." At the end of his life, he was invited to join the staff of the London 'Morning Chronicle', but by then he was too ill to move over the door. Had he been able, there is no doubt his choice of vocation would have been as a poet and folklorist. His genius lay in his song writing ability. Had he been allowed, he would have happily given the rest of his life to rescuing and refurbishing old songs, to send them out refreshed into the world as works of lyric art. But perhaps one should not dwell on what he might have done, but only be grateful for what he did in fact achieve.

The Glasgow Herald.

DAILY.   TUESDAY, SEPTEMBER 23, 1862.

...... exertions of the milit....

At the present moment the Government of Mr. Lincoln is sorely puzzled with a superabundance of "contraband" and emancipated negroes. They are everywhere present in the land, and in the President's calculations; and how they are to be accommodated or got rid of is the perplexing question. They have been seriously advised to take themselves off quietly, and found colonies or kingdoms somewhere, as soon as they can find time, space, and opportunity, providing always that the locality is outside of the United States. Mr. Lincoln has plainly intimated to the free coloured people of the North that they are an inferior race, and that white men, as a general rule, are better pleased with their absence than their company. He feels sincerely for their helpless and almost hopeless position in the North; and while he is ready enough to admit their many good qualities, he wishes them to make "tracks" across the border as soon as convenient. To many people this policy may appear to be selfish and somewhat unnatural, but Mr. Lincoln is not to be blamed for stating the simple truth. It is notorious that Americans, native and imported, have a deep-rooted dislike of the negro population in the North, and no process of reasoning seems capable of transforming that feeling into anything stronger than simple toleration. And this prejudice against the African race is not confined to Democrats, "Free-soilers," or other classes of politicians; for the most extreme Abolitionists love the poor "niggers"

far better when they are kept at a respectable distance. In these circumstances, the advice of President Lincoln is doubtless given to the coloured people with the very best intentions regarding their future welfare; but the misfortune is, that it seems to be impracticable. It is very easy to theorise on schemes of colonisation in distant lands, where perfect Arcadias might be formed, and where servitude and scorn would trouble the Africans no more. It is altogether a very different thing, however, to put these theories into a practical shape, and reduce them to the ordeal and necessities of every-day life. In the first place, where are these poor people to go, and how are they to be transported to their new homes when found? Mr. Lincoln promises material assistance for this purpose, but at present the Federal Government has little funds to spare for anything but war. In all likelihood, therefore, the negro colonisation scheme will be shelved until the advent of a more convenient season, if the future has such a thing in store for the statesmen at Washington.

But although there is little hope of .... plans being reduced to pract.....
..... emigrat....

> 'My ancient but ignoble blood,
> Has crept through scoundrels since the flood.'

At eighteen years of age, he described himself in his Commonplace Book as: 'Robert Burnes, a man who has little art in making money, still less in keeping it; but is, however, a man of some sense, a great deal of honesty, and unbounded good will to every creature'. Burns was obsessed with the individuality of man. He was conscious of his own uniqueness and recognised the same in all humanity. He resented any denigration of human dignity and status, and saw in such acts an insult to God, in whose image man was made. He saw, too, that many of his fellow-men were in a condition of perpetual slavery, not only in the literal sense, as with his African brothers and their American cousins, but in his own countrymen's bondage in a wider sense. In the way they were tied to their station in life, to the jobs they held, to their ambitions and desires, to their appetites, and to their general apathy and lack of will, they too were slaves, just as if they had been branded and chained. So many accepted dumbly the level they were accorded without ever wishing to do anything about it. For his part, he was never averse to giving fate a nudge and helping it on its way. He always had an eye out for the main chance, but circumstances never allowed him to take any advantage from his acuity. He made many friends in high places, ever willing to help, but then he would say the wrong thing at exactly the right time, and the helping hands would be swiftly withdrawn. In many of his letters, expertly penned, subtlely couched, he sought to find ways and means to better his condition and free himself from the 'slavery' of his own state. Even into his last hours, he was still working at surviving. In fact, his last words were a mumbled reference to a bill he owed a tailor. Yet he had refused to sell a song to George Thomson's Select Collection, but gave it to him free, considering that such songs belonged to everyone. However, at the very end he was forced to sell, promising the publisher 'five pounds worth of the neatest song-writing'. Thomson sent the money. But it was too late.

Excerpt from

O Man! while in thy early years,
   How prodigal of time!
Mispending all thy precious hours,
   Thy glorious, youthful prime!
Alternate Follies take the sway!
   Licentious Passions burn;
Which tenfold force gives Nature's law,
   That Man was made to mourn.

Look not alone on youthful Prime,
   Or Manhood's, active might;
Man then is useful to his kind,
   Supported is his right:
But see him on the edge of life,
   With Cares and Sorrows worn,
Then Age and Want, Oh! ill-match'd pair!
   Show Man was made to mourn.

A few seem favourites of Fate,
   In Pleasure's lap carest;
Yet, think not all the Rich and Great,
   Are likewise truly blest.
But Oh, what crouds in ev'ry land,
   All wretched and forlorn,
Thro' weary life this lesson learn,
   That Man was made to mourn!

Many and sharp the num'rous Ills
   Inwoven with our frame!
More pointed still we make ourselves,
   Regret, Remorse and Shame!
And Man, whose heav'n–erected face,
   The smiles of love adorn,
Man's inhumanity to Man
   Makes countless thousands mourn!

See, yonder poor, o'erlabour'd wight,
   So abject, mean and vile,
Who begs a brother of the earth
   To give him leave to toil;
And see his lordly *fellow-worm,*
   The poor petition spurn,
Unmindful, tho' a weeping wife,
   And helpless offspring mourn.

If I'm design'd yon lordling's slave,
   By Nature's law design'd,
Why was an independent wish
   E'er planted in my mind?
If not, why am I subject to
   His cruelty, or scorn?
Or why has Man the will and pow'r
   To make his fellow mourn?

'O, why has worth so short a date,
While villains ripen grey with time?'

He was never given time to win totally clear of his station, but even within his allotted span, he trumpeted the claims of singular man in a sad world, and reserved the right to speak out on his behalf. Though he was, on occasions, obliged to tug the forelock, his independent mind was always his own.

'Lord, what is man? What a bustling little bundle of passions, ideas and fancies . . . But lately I was a boy, more recently a youth, and now, though I've not lived half the life of an old man, I feel the grip of age stiffening in all my joints . . . What a business is this life.'

The Glasgow Herald.

PUBLISHED DAILY.   THURSDAY, JUNE 8, 1871.   PRICE ONE

GLASGOW AND WEST OF SCOTLAND HORTICULTURAL SOCIETY.

The second show of the season, held in the City Hall yesterday, under the auspices of this society, was of a meritorious character. Seldom have we seen the art of the horticulturist so effectively displayed throughout as in the specimens of flowering and beautiful leaved plants placed upon the tables for competition and exhibition. Usually we have some of the good and some little of the indifferent in cultivation commingled, and to the uninitiated eye the whole seems very respectable; but connoisseurs look askance at this state of matters, and call aloud for the science or art, at least in connection with the objects of nature, to be represented in its best habiliments. To those, and such as those, there was little to complain of. The true naturalist sees some beauty in every flower, and cannot subscribe to the notion that "there is nought in nature bright, where roses do not shed their light." That is a reason why we should complain in some measure that Pomona should be so meagrely represented in the West of Scotland. Why, for example, was there only one solitary dish of grapes upon the table? It cannot be that the gardens of the noble and the wealthy have not that choice fruit in season just now, else we should say pomiculture was retrogressing in the West of Scotland when it is progressing everywhere else. The flowering plants and the flowers generally, however, made up for the deficiency, and the promenaders, as usual, seemed to be delighted with "The Flower Show," and the splendid music that was discoursed by the band of the Scots Greys. The day was auspicious, and the attendance, not quite so numerous at the select hours, increased to a throng in the afternoon and evening.

We have already commented upon the horticultural character of the articles exhibited, and we have now a word in favour of the pleasing tout ensemble presented by the arrangement. This is a matter of great moment. The prize tables of plants were improved in this point of view. Prominent among the exhibitors was Mr Thomas Coats of Ferguslie, Paisley, who, as usual, contributed many choice specimens of the richest exotic flora. His table was put up by Mr Dickson with great taste, and elicited much admiration. Centred as it was with that beautiful fair palm Livistona borbonica, and that equally ornamental species of the same order, Cyathea dealbata, with great arching fronds, silver looking underneath, it contrasted well with the elliptic-leaved Diospyros, and formed splendid relief subjects for the varied lesser grown plants with which they were associated. Chief among them in point of interest was the pure waxy white flowered Stephanotis floribunda, which is so eligible and in such demand for the rarest of brides' bouquets; then numerous orchids, which exceed in beauty or interest the whole of the floral race, chief among them being the Indian Saccolabrium retusum, with racemes of flowers so close set upon the stem as to resemble a fox brush. Along with this let us name the grand showy flowering Cattleya mossiæ, the equally ornate Brazilian Lælia purpurata, the New Grenadan Anguloa Clowesii, &c. These, interspersed with ferns and fine foliaged and flowering plants, made up a most effective table of miscellaneous plants.

Chief among competitors was Peter Denny, of Helenslee. His gardener, Mr Sutherland, certainly staged some as highly cultivated plants as ever we have seen upon the competition tables in the City Hall. His crotons were marvellous specimens of art, and quite unexceptional in point of health. In fact, no plant, of any country or kind, could match, for ornament, these great pyramids of gold and green, and white and gold, and bronze and russet colours. No gentleman could cultivate a better class of plants than these, and they were well supported with good flowered azaleas. One, "Flower of the Day," was quite a picture of snow-white beauty. We must also specially note the umbelliferous heads of scarlet ixoras, set upon fine green ovate foliage, which looked more than handsome; while the heads gave tone and variety to the contributions. One, named Coccinea minor, was a great beauty, and met you in a variety of classes throughout the two halls where the plants were shown. This exhibitor took position in a great many classes, as can be seen from the prize list, and all his plants were well handled. We must particularly notify the collection of ferns, which was one of the very best we have seen exhibited anywhere in this country for style and beauty. The forms of gold and lispid ferns, along with the New Zealand Todea superba, were quite entrancing, and many ladies admired them in their promenade. Mr David Tod sent a very fine assortment, which was well put up by Mr Hogg; and Mr Andrew Bannatyne had so good a lot that the judges could not separate the distinction of merit between that and Mr Tod's, and so an equal second prize was awarded: Mr T. D. Findlay, Easterhill, had a very fine lot of plants, which ran Mr Denny's so hard that the judges had much difficulty in discriminating between them, but eventually the palm was awarded to Mr Denny. Mrs Orem, The Rookes, had a very superior lot of plants, creditable to Mr Murray; but they lacked the size and wanted the variety of Mr Denny's lot, although one of the plants—Erica Victoria—was selected, and deservedly so, as the most meritorious plant in the whole exhibition. This was one of the best managed heaths we ever saw, and was in folly or great style as when shown last year, to receive the same distinguished honour. Can no competitor out-match this specimen, that has become so distinguished?

Coming to ... ... of plants, we have ... Stewart ...

Extract from a letter to Mrs Dunlop:

'We know nothing or next to nothing of the substance or structure of our souls, so cannot account for those seeming caprices in them, that one should be particularly pleased with this thing, or struck with that. I have some favourite flowers in spring, the mountain daisy, the harebell, the foxglove, the wild briar rose and the hawthorn. I never hear the solitary whistle of a curlew on a summer noon, or the wild mixing cadence of a troop of grey plovers on a summer morning, without feeling an elevation of the soul, like an enthusiasm of devotion. To what can this be owing? Are we a piece of machinery, which like the Aeolian harp, passive, takes the impression of the passing accident? Or do these workings argue within us something above the trodden clod? I own myself partial to such proofs of those awful and important realities—a God that made all things—man's immaterial and immortal nature—and a world of weal and woe beyond death and the grave.'

Burns was a devoted and lifelong student at the College of Nature, and might be said to have graduated 'cum lauda' from the University of Life.

To a Mountain-Daisy,
On turning one down, with the Plough, in April—1786

Excerpt from

Wee, modest, crimson-tipped flow'r,
Thou's met me in an evil hour;
For I maun crush amang the stoure
      Thy slender stem:
To spare thee now is past my pow'r,
      Thou bonie gem.

Cauld blew the bitter-biting *North*
Upon thy early, humble birth;
Yet chearfully thou glinted forth
      Amid the storm,
Scarce rear'd above the *Parent-earth*
      Thy tender form.

The flaunting *flow'rs* our Gardens yield,
High-shelt'ring woods and wa's maun shield,
But thou, beneath the random bield
      O' clod or stane,
Adorns the histie *stibble-field,*
      Unseen, alane.

There, in thy scanty mantle clad,
Thy snawie bosom sun-ward spread,
Thou lifts thy unassuming head
      In humble guise;
But now the *share* uptears thy bed,
      And low thou lies!

Such is the fate of artless Maid,
Sweet *flow'ret* of the rural shade!
By Love's simplicity betray'd,
      And guileless trust,
Till she, like thee, all soil'd, is laid
      Low i' the dust.

'Gie me a spark o' nature's fire,
That's a' the learning I desire.'

He never tired of observing nature throughout its different seasons, and could detect all the colours in its complicated canvas. His devotion to flowers and growing things was quite real, as was his ear for birdsong and the soothing tranquility of twilight at the end of the day. These things meant more to him than the artificiality of the Edinburgh salon, Senor Urbani's orchestral trills, or the arid chill of a typical Kirk service. He was aware of the reality all about him, and saw his fellow-man within the context of the natural world. Any trivial exhibition, trite display, or pompous monument was anathema to him. He would surely have been appalled at the number of statues raised in his image all over the world, the frequency of his likenesses on cake tins and chocolate boxes. This is the Burns industry, not the Burns identity. If he is to be found, he is there in his work, every line of which is redolent with the images and likenesses that inspired him—the rush of Afton water, the still beauty of Cumnock valley as it was then, the birks at Aberfeldy, the falls at Bruar, the banks of the River Doon, and all the other natural spectacles he had stored in his mind till he could set them on the page. To him, the free gifts of nature were the prime treasures of life and available to the ordinary man. He never ceased to sing its joys, nor exult in its many manifestations. Every blade of grass, every leaf on a tree, and even a twig from the hedgerow had a meaning for him. They were rooted and had their being in the same world he lived in. He wanted to celebrate that life.

The Glasgow Herald.

EAR.—No. 194.   PUBLISHED DAILY.   FRIDAY, AUGUST 14, 1885.   PRICE

It seems that, contrary to many expectations, the Duke of Richmond and Gordon, the present President of the Board of Trade, is to be the first Secretary for Scotland. The Bill creating that office has become law, and we are not sure that the Conservatives have made a bad stroke in appointing so distinguished a nobleman and good man of business to fill it. The appointment no doubt comes rather as a surprise. We should hardly have thought that the Duke of Richmond and Gordon would have cared to accept such a position. It was generally thought that one of the younger Lords on the Conservative side would have been asked to fill the place, a Scotchman who, by his thorough knowledge of Scottish affairs and manner of thought, might have been considered well fitted to fill the office. Lord Balfour of Burleigh, for example, is a thoroughly good Scotchman, with a considerable knowledge of Scottish education, and, perhaps, with a fair proportion of Scottish prejudices. But possibly Lord Balfour disqualified himself by speaking strongly, as an educationalist like himself was bound to do, against the inclusion of education among the many duties of the Scottish Secretary. The Marquis of Lothian was another probable candidate for the office, and there was no disqualification in this respect on his part. But neither of these two noblemen, both of them able and deserving men and Scottish politicians, could have claimed to take the position in Scotland of that occupied by Lord Rosebery, who, if the Liberals had been in power, would no doubt have been our first Secretary. Neither, for that matter, can it be said that the Duke of Richmond and Gordon is able to claim the same confidence and regard as the laird of Dalmeny. But the Duke is a great nobleman, he has large estates in Scotland, and in a different way as compared with Lord Rosebery is highly respected as a man of business and sound common-sense, whose presence as Chairman of a Committee of the House of Lords on a Private Bill is always considered by those interested as a fortunate circumstance.

One thing is almost certain, and that is that the Duke will commit no egregious blunder, nor is he likely to assert to any extreme extent his powers as the Secretary for the northern kingdom. He will do his work modestly and efficiently and with the minimum amount of oratory, the latter always to be considered as a virtue in an administrator. The Duke of Richmond and Gordon as Scottish Secretary will, of course, be a member of the Conservative Cabinet. With regard to the educational part of his duties, as a Vice-President of the Council, and practical chief of primary education in Scotland, the Duke has had a lengthened experience in educational matters, having been President of the Council under Lord Beaconsfield's last Administration. It may be fairly presumed that he knows well the educational relationships of both countries, and is not likely to seek to disturb them in so far as they work harmoniously together. Upon the whole, the people of Scotland may be congratulated that, since the fates have so ordered that Lord Rosebery is not to be our first Scottish Secretary, the position is to be filled by so distinguished a nobleman and really good man as the Duke of Richmond and Gordon. Lord Salisbury has acted with his usual shrewdness and political insight. His Grace will naturally dignify the newly-created Secretaryship, and his character as a statesman will give confidence to the people of Scotland. His appointment is a surprise, but it is an agreeable one.

'In politics if you would mix,
And mean your fortunes be;
Bear this in mind, be deaf and blind,
Let great folks hear and see.'

These were lines written on one of the windows of the Globe Tavern in Dumfries. Burns had a penchant for etching rhymes in this manner, even if his discretion did not always match his cryptic verse skills. If he were a politician at all, he was essentially a pragmatic one. He saw very well how the world worked and the way the wheels turned, and however indignant he waxed at the machinations of the politicians, he was little attracted to take any part himself. He was asked about standing for Parliament but refused out of hand. Influential gentlemen were quite keen to harness his charisma and obvious public appeal, but he had no wish to go to London. If he felt that the Scottish capital was an artificial environment, what would he have made of the capital of England? One is tempted however to consider that had Burns gone to the House of Commons then, he would have come into collision with Edmund Burke. What verbal fireworks these gifted orators might have created, although it must be said Burns' was of a more conversational nature. In fact, this was the quality about him which most impressed Maria Riddell. How he achieved this high degree of articulation can only be ascribed to his father's earnest insistence that he should

Fareweel to a' our Scottish fame,
   Fareweel our ancient glory;
Fareweel even to the Scottish name,
   Sae fam'd in martial story!
Now Sark rins o'er the Solway sands,
   And Tweed rins to the ocean,
To mark whare England's province stands,
   Such a parcel of rogues in a nation!

What force or guile could not subdue,
   Thro' many warlike ages,
Is wrought now by a coward few,
   For hireling traitors' wages.
The English steel we could disdain,
   Secure in valor's station;
But English gold has been our bane,
   Such a parcel of rogues in a nation!

O would, or I had seen the day
   That treason thus could sell us,
My auld grey head had lien in clay,
   Wi' Bruce and loyal Wallace!
But pith and power, till my last hour,
   I'll mak this declaration;
We're bought and sold for English gold,
   Such a parcel of rogues in a nation!

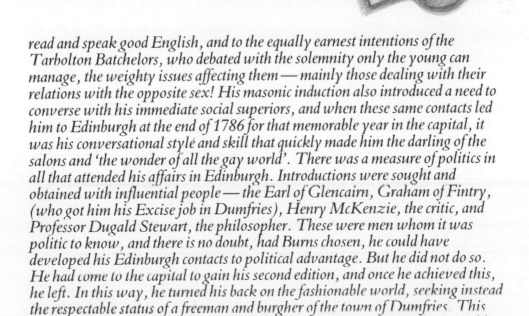

read and speak good English, and to the equally earnest intentions of the Tarbolton Batchelors, who debated with the solemnity only the young can manage, the weighty issues affecting them — mainly those dealing with their relations with the opposite sex! His masonic induction also introduced a need to converse with his immediate social superiors, and when these same contacts led him to Edinburgh at the end of 1786 for that memorable year in the capital, it was his conversational style and skill that quickly made him the darling of the salons and 'the wonder of all the gay world'. There was a measure of politics in all that attended his affairs in Edinburgh. Introductions were sought and obtained with influential people — the Earl of Glencairn, Graham of Fintry, (who got him his Excise job in Dumfries), Henry McKenzie, the critic, and Professor Dugald Stewart, the philosopher. These were men whom it was politic to know, and there is no doubt, had Burns chosen, he could have developed his Edinburgh contacts to political advantage. But he did not do so. He had come to the capital to gain his second edition, and once he achieved this, he left. In this way, he turned his back on the fashionable world, seeking instead the respectable status of a freeman and burgher of the town of Dumfries. This was not the decision of a careerist, but of a man who knew his mind. He could not sincerely give himself to either party, Whig or Tory. He was his own party — his own man.

The Glasgow Herald.

YEAR.—No. 253.　*WITH SUPPLEMENT.*　WEDNESDAY, OCTOBER 22, 1890.　*TWELVE PAGES.*　PRICE ONE PENNY.

MADAME SARAH BERNHARDT AS CLEOPATRA.

DESCRIPTIVE ACCOUNT OF THE PLAY.

(FROM OUR SPECIAL CORRESPONDENT.)

Paris, October 21.

I learn that the dress rehearsal of Sardou's version of "Cleopatra" takes place to-morrow at the Porte Saint Martin, and the first public performance on Thursday. The event is awaited with the greatest interest. The mounting of the play is marvellous, the cost of production being not less than £12,000. It is possible that a good deal that has been expected, such as the use of real snakes from Fontainebleau, will not be given. I am in a position to give you in advance the complete plot of the play.

The incidental music of the piece is composed by M. Xavier Leroux, who carried off the Prix de Rome five years ago, and is now a pupil of M. Massenet. It is original and striking, and shews that that young man has considerable talent. In the first scene a flourish of sounds is produced by trumpets and trombones. Then comes Cleopatra, and the Oriental colour of her entry is obtained by a combination of flutes, oboes, harps, mutels, sistrums, and tambourines. The opening bars are a bright, cheerful march, and this is succeeded by a melodious phrase in A major, executed on flutes, clarinettes, and oboes. Presently choral voices are heard mingling in a quartette, and the whole joining into the instrumentation of the beginning, gives the morceau an effect that is sweet and full of melancholy colouring. Music of the same sort precedes Cleopatra's exit with Antony.

The first number in the second act, a ballet et buffoons, is a wild sort of comical rhythm, in which the thumping of tomtoms comes in from time to time, while towards the end the refrain is accompanied by xylophones, bells, and cymbals. The second number is a series of variations on a melody of Oriental colour, the first variation being exclusively accompanied by tambourines and cymbals, and the whole serves as accompaniment to a sort of sacred dance, in the midst of which are heard voices that excite the feelings of the priestesses, who become gradually more and more impassioned by the sound of gongs and human cries, and finish their dance in an eddying whirl as the choruses chaunt the sacred names of Egypt's gods. The interlude, in D flat, that follows this ballet is executed by the quartetto and harps, and there is an alto solo. The style of this music is that which suits Oriental legends. It is a kind of sweet, melodious phrasing of from eight to ten measures, which are regularly broken by a like refrain on zithers, harps, mutels, flutes, and a cymbal. It is wholly descriptive, and I think follows well both the text and the pantomimic play of Sarah Bernhardt.

In Act III. a chorus of women pass along the banks of the Nile to an accompaniment of harps and flutes. This morceau, written in B major, has no precise tonality, as it is completely composed on an Oriental major gamut, raised, however, two tones above that key. It is strange music, and accords with the scenic surroundings of pyramids and sphinxes. The flourishing of Roman and Egyptian trumpets are frequently heard alternating and responding to each other.

In the fourth act, and then in the fifth, we have two incidental episodes originating in the Temple of Typhon, where priests are praying. The invocation to Typhon, preceded by a march of priests and priestesses to the accompaniment of harps and flutes, is interrupted by the rumbling of distant thunder, but it is only when the march is finished and the procession coming out of the temple is on the stage that the invocation begins; meanwhile the choruses respond to Cleopatra by repeating the strophes she declaims. This invocation is at first heavy, grave, and slow. It increases in quickness gradually, and while the orchestra symphonically develops the tempest that is rising, the chorus go on augmenting little by little in intensity until at last the whole terminates in the midst of flashes of lightning and in magnificent volumes of sound. Finally, in the last scene of this act, there is an interlude during the death of Antony and of Cleopatra, which incidental morceau is composed of a fragment of the priestly prayers in the preceding scene and by the interlude in D flat of the second act.

The complete cast of all the parts is as follows :—

Cleopatra	Mmes.	Sarah Bernhardt.
Octavie	"	Laure Fleur.
Iras	"	Lemark.
Charmion	"	Simonton.
A Young Slave	"	Lacroix.
Mark Antony	Messrs	Philippe Garnier.
Demetrius	"	Bouyer.
Kephren	"	Durmont.
Dercetas	"	Rebel.
Thyrsus	"	Lacroix.
Olympos	"	Romy.
A Messenger	"	Herbert.
Delius	"	Denneboucq.
Octavius	"	Desche.

When John Murdoch was engaged by William Burnes to tutor Robert and Gilbert in Grammar and English Literature, he had occasion to stay overnight. After supper, he read to the assembled family Shakespeare's tragedy of 'Titus Andronicus'. According to Gilbert, Robert was so incensed with the plot that he would not hear it out, and threatened to throw the book on the fire. Murdoch hurriedly changed to 'The School for Love' (translated from the French). In this way, Burns indicated his preferences early, and showed that he had very definite views as a critic! There is no record of his ever having seen a play in Ayrshire. However, on his Edinburgh visits, among the people he met was the Scottish 'Roscius'—the actor William Woods. Indeed, it was from Woods' coach that Burns fell and wrenched his knee. Both said it was the driver who was drunk! In 1787, Burns wrote the prologue for Woods to speak on his Benefit Night, and seemed to understand well the actor's particular problem in playing to a Scottish audience:

'Poor is the task to please a barb'rous throng
It needs no Siddon's powers in Southern's song;
But here an ancient nation fam'd afar
For genius, learning high, as great in war—
Hail Caledonia, name for ever dear!
Before whose sons I'm honoured to appear . . .'

As soon as Burns had taken up house in Dumfries there were immediate references to his being at the Theatre Royal in Shakespeare St. to see the play. He was present during the notorious 'Ca Ira' disturbances in the theatre at the time of the French threat. It was reported that he sat through the playing of 'God Save the King' with his hat on and his arms folded. Right from the beginning of his Dumfries days he was marked as a putative rebel and unashamed nonconformist. It was no surprise that the theatricals embraced him,

Scots Prologue, For Mrs. Sutherland's Benefit Night, Spoken at the Theatre Dumfries

What needs this din about the town o' Lon'on?
How this new Play, and that new Sang is comin?
Why is outlandish stuff sae meikle courted?
Does Nonsense mend, like Brandy, when imported–
Is there nae Poet, burning keen for Fame,
Will bauldly try to gie us Plays at hame?
For Comedy abroad he need na toil,
A Knave an' Fool are plants of ev'ry soil:
Nor need he hunt as far as Rome or Greece,
To gather matter for a serious piece;
There's themes enow in Caledonian story,
Wad shew the Tragic Muse in a' her glory.
Is there no daring Bard will rise and tell
How glorious Wallace stood, how hapless fell?
Where are the Muses fled, that should produce
A *drama* worthy of the name of Bruce?
How on *this* spot he first unsheath'd the sword
'Gainst mighty England and her guilty Lord,
And after many a bloody, deathless doing,
Wrench'd his dear country from the jaws of Ruin!
O! for a Shakespeare or an Otway scene,
To paint the lovely hapless Scottish Queen!
Vain ev'n the omnipotence of Female charms,
'Gainst headlong, ruthless, mad Rebellion's arms.
She fell—but fell with spirit truly Roman,
To glut that direst foe,—*a vengeful woman;*
A *woman*—tho' the phrase may seem uncivil,
As able—and as wicked as the devil!
(One Douglas lives in Home's immortal page,
But Douglases were heroes every age:
And tho' your fathers, prodigal of life,
A Douglas followed to the martial strife,
Perhaps, if bowls row right, and Right succeeds,
Ye yet may follow where a Douglas leads!)

As ye have generous done, if a' the land
Would take the Muses' servants by the hand,
Not only hear—but patronise—defend them,
And where ye justly can commend—commend them;
And aiblins when they winna stand the test,
Wink hard and say, 'The folks hae done their best.'
Would 'a the land do this, then I'll be caition,
Ye'll soon hae Poets o' the Scottish nation,
Will gar Fame blaw until her trumpet crack,
And warsle Time, and lay him on his back.

For us and for our Stage, should only spier,
'Whase aught thae Chiels maks a' this bustle here?'
My best leg foremost, I'll set up my brow,
We have the honor to belong to you!
We're your ain bairns, e'en guide us as ye like,
But, like guid mothers, shore before ye strike;
And grateful still, I trust, ye'll ever find us:
For gen'rous patronage, and meikle kindness,
We've got frae a' professions, sorts, an' ranks:
God help us!—we're but poor—ye 'se get but thanks!

and that he felt so easy in their gypsy company. In 1790, he wrote to his brother Gilbert: "We have gotten a set of very decent players here just now. I have seen them an evening or two. David Campbell of Ayr wrote me by the manager of the company, a Mr Sutherland, who indeed is a man of genius and apparent worth." Burns wrote several prologues for Sutherland and his wife and was on the Free List for the theatre. He also admired one of the actresses, Louisa Fontenelle, to whom he sent a poem—'On Seeing Her in a Favourite Character':

'Wert thou awkward, stiff, affected,
Spurning nature, torturing art,
Loves and graces all rejected,
Then, indeed, thou'dst act a part.'

For her, too, he wrote 'The Rights of Women' which she spoke on her Benefit Night in 1792. What a pity he never wrote a play. He had a natural theatrical instinct as his narrative writing showed, and as 'The Jolly Beggars' teasingly hinted.

The Glasgow Herald.

119TH YEAR.—No. 20. WEDNESDAY, JANUARY 23, 1901. FOURTEEN PAGES. PRICE ONE PENNY.

SUITABLE MATERIALS
FOR MOURNINGS, IN ALMOST ENDLESS VARIETY,
AT
JOHN ANDERSON'S
ROYAL POLYTECHNIC, LTD.
BLACK SILKS.
SPECIAL VALUE.
COMTAULD'S CREPES.
ALL QUALITIES.
BLACK MATERIALS
IN EVERY MAKE.
BLACK RIBBONS.
ALL WIDTHS.
FOR GOOD QUALITY, COMBINED WITH VALUE, YOU CAN'T BEAT THE POLYTECHNIC.
BLACK CREPE SCARFS,
1s 11d, 2s 6½d, 2s 11d, 3s 11d, to 5s 11d Each.
MOURNING HANDKERCHIEFS,
1s 11d, 2s 11d, 3s 11d, 5s 11d, to 7s 11d per Half-Dozen.
MOURNING HAT BANDS,
MOURNING ARM BANDS,
GLOVES FOR MOURNING, &c., &c.
MILLINERY FOR MOURNING
A SPECIALITY.
BLACK DRAPING CLOTH
FOR CHURCHES AND PUBLIC BUILDINGS.
RICH BLACK SILKS.
EVERY REQUISITE FOR COMPLIMENTARY WEAR.

RICH BLACK PEAU DE SOIE,
2s 6d, 3s 11d, 4s 11d, 5s 11d per yard.
RICH BLACK SATIN DUCHESSE.
All Silk, 3s 6½d, 4s 11d, to 7s 11d per yard.
RICH BLACK BROCHE SILK,
2s 11½d, 3s 11d, 4s 11d.
ALSO,
A SPECIAL LOT OF BONNET SILKS,
6s 11D PER YARD.
RICH BLACK GROS GRAINS,
2s 6D, 3s 6D, TO 5s 11D PER YARD.
RICH BLACK SATIN MERV,
1s 6½D TO 4s 11D PER YARD—ALL PURE SILK.
DRESSMAKING DEPARTMENT.
UNDER THE MANAGEMENT OF A THOROUGHLY EXPERIENCED HIGH-CLASS DRESSMAKER.
COMFORTABLE FITTING-ROOMS.
CUT AND STYLE GUARANTEED.
JOHN ANDERSON,
ROYAL POLYTECHNIC, LTD.,
97 ARGYLL STREET.

Burns had no fear of death. "What is there to fear?" he said. "If in our lives we have been the sport of instincts, we go to a God who gave us these instincts and well knows their force." He also said, "Folk maun dae somethin' for their breid, and sae maun death." Burns personalised death in the figure of Satan, Clootie, Auld Nick, or Auld Hornie, whichever appellation came to mind. He had been near death himself so many times, it was almost become a familiar. He met the prospect first at Lochlea, and again at Irvine, where he composed 'A Prayer in the Prospect of Death'. On his Border and Highland Tours, he was attacked by severe colitis, or colic, as he called it. Finally rheumatism and arthritis heralded the slow decline into death at Dumfries. To the end he was realistic. "My life reminds me of a ruined temple; what proportion in some parts, what unsightly gaps, what prostrate ruin in others." Of the death, his son, Robert, was to write, "At five o'clock in the morning, we children were summoned to look upon our father for the last time. After some delirium, he sank into a calm repose. His last words were something about a bill he owed a tailor." When he passed away on the morning of the 21st July, there was a loud moaning from the people on the street. The children could not understand. To them their father was not a famous man. He was their father. The largest crowd ever seen in the town gathered for the funeral. It was almost as if Dumfries couldn't wait for him to die, so that they could bury him in style. He had been an uncomfortable figure to them while he was alive, even though he was their

Excerpt from

Why am I loth to leave this earthly scene?
  Have I so found it full of pleasing charms?
Some drops of joy with draughts of ill between;
  Some gleams of sunshine mid renewing storms:
Is it departing pangs my soul alarms?
  Or Death's unlovely, dreary, dark abode?
For guilt, for guilt, my terrors are in arms;
  I tremble to approach an angry God,
And justly smart beneath his sin-avenging rod.

Fain would I say, "Forgive my foul offence!"
  Fain promise never more to disobey;
But, should my Author health again dispense,
  Again I might desert fair Virtue's way;
  Again in Folly's path might go astray;
  Again exalt the brute and sink the man;
Then how should I for Heavenly Mercy pray,
  Who act so counter Heavenly Mercy's plan?
Who sin so oft have mourn'd, yet to temptation ran?

most famous citizen. But dead he could be safely dealt with. He was at first buried in a poor man's grave, then hurriedly disinterred when his death made such a noise throughout Britain, even in faraway London. It is said that when the gravediggers dug him up at the dead of night, his head came away from his body. They had to scrabble in the dark to find it. When they did, his sable hair had turned quite grey! Now Scotland could comfortably forget the man, and concentrate on his 'immortal' memory. A subscription list was immediately set up for a mausoleum to mark the memory of the works of Burns, (not, one notes, to the man) and to make some provision for Jean and her young family — especially since her son, Maxwell, had been born on the 25th July, the very day of his father's funeral. When the mausoleum was finally erected at a cost of fifteen hundred pounds, to the design of Mr. T. S. Hunt, it left around seven hundred pounds for the family. It was quite forgotten that Burns had died worrying about being pressed for a trivial little account! As Wordsworth said, "Poor Burns, he had asked for bread, and they gave him a stone!"

The Glasgow Herald.

132nd YEAR—No. 186.   WEDNESDAY, AUGUST 5, 1914.   TWELVE PAGES, ONE PENNY.

BRITAIN'S DECISIVE HOUR.

WAR WITH GERMANY PROCLAIMED

All Military Forces Called Out.

Government Take Over Railways.

THE NATION'S PATRIOTISM

Great Britain declared war on Germany at eleven o'clock last night.

An Ultimatum was yesterday sent to Germany demanding a reply within 12 hours.

That Ultimatum expired at midnight, before which hour an unsatisfactory reply was received.

The whole of the military forces in the country, including the Territorials, have been called out, and the Government have taken over the railways.

THE DECLARATION.

We are authorised by the Foreign Office to publish the following official statement :—

Owing to the summary rejection by the German Government of the request made by His Majesty's Government for assurances that the neutrality of Belgium will be respected, His Majesty's Ambassador to Berlin has received his passports, and His Majesty's Government declared to the German Government that a state of war exists between Great Britain and Germany as from 11 p.m. on August 4.

His attitude to war was, for the most part, romantic, rather than practical. His famous pragmatism hardly applied in his reaction to contemporary affairs among the nations. It was only reluctantly that he joined the Dumfries Volunteers. In fact, he only wore the red uniform once, but friends thought it was a necessary political move, given Burns' indiscreet statements around that time. He was forever the paradox. Hailed as a hero on one day for helping to capture the French schooner, Rosemonde, as she lay off the Solway, it is said that on the next, he was castigated as a traitor for buying the ship's guns at the quay auction, and returning them to the French with his compliments. It was no doubt the act of a poet, but it was hardly that of a government servant in wartime. Fortunately, powerful influences saved him from disgrace once again. He had a proper patriotic spirit, but his fervour applied more to the Scottish soldier in history than to the poor mercenary and press-ganged sailor of his own

The Dumfries Volunteers

Does haughty Gaul invasion threat,
  Then let the louns bewaure, Sir,
There's Wooden Walls upon our seas,
  And Volunteers on shore, Sir:
The *Nith* shall run to *Corsincon*,
  And *Criffell* sink in *Solway*,
E'er we permit a Foreign Foe
  On British ground to rally.

O, let us not, like snarling tykes,
  In wrangling be divided,
Till, slap! come in an *unco loun*,
  And wi' a rung decide it!
Be Britain still to Britain true,
  Amang oursels united;
For never but by British hands
  Must British wrongs be righted.

The wretch that would a *Tyrant* own,
  And the wretch, his true–sworn brother,
Who'd set the *Mob* above the *Throne*,
  May they be damn'd together!
Who will not sing, God Save the King,
  Shall hang as high 's the steeple;
But while we sing, God Save the King,
  We'll ne'er forget The People!

day. War was ancient battles to him, and not contemporaneous manoeuvres. He preferred war as a tale of old heroics and not, as he knew it really was, a catalogue of lost limbs and the wailing grief of widows. Like any artist, like any man of sensibility, he could never condone war, and yet like any citizen, he was required from time to time, to make at least a gesture of compliance and conformity. As he wrote to Clarinda, "When matters are desperate, we must put on a desperate face." He was forced as a prominent public man to make the appropriate noises. He realised, as any thinking man would, that war, however great, came down to one man coldly killing another, and this he could never countenance. He owned a brace of pistols, but it was only as part of his exciseman's equipment. He carried a sword, but it was only as a parade item with the *Dumfries Volunteers*. Burns did not depend for his manliness on martiality, and it was only in a Cantata, like 'Love and Liberty', that he could admire his Jolly Beggars romping freely in Pussy Nancie's and strutting like 'sodger laddies' and 'braw, braw Hielanmen'. The Highland Regiments were already being formed from the displaced clansmen to fight the Englishman's battles for him and to begin the territorial plundering that became the British Empire. The Scots were being dragooned to fight England's wars, and he would have nothing of that. Burns never lost sight of the personal element of wars, especially in the private area. The common soldier was his concern more than the general's glory.

> 'The brave poor sodger ne'er despise,
> Nor count him as a stranger;
> Remember he's his country's stay,
> In day and hour of danger.'

The Glasgow Herald

144th YEAR—No. 144   THURSDAY, JUNE 17, 1926.   TWOPENCE

THE READING HABIT

TASK OF THE LIBRARIAN

LOST TO EDUCATIONAL INFLUENCE

Speaking at the annual meeting of the Scottish Library Association which was held at Perth yesterday, the president, Mr Ryrie Orr, F.E.I.S., Greenock, said that in every three years there were more than a million children leaving school at the age of fourteen who were lost to educational influence.

There was no more crying need in the country to-day than the further education of these children, and it was to them that the libraries opened their doors.

A CRYING NEED

A large number of delegates from all parts of Scotland were present. The delegates were extended a civic welcome by Lord Provost Dempster, and the Magistrates, and Mr Ryrie Orr replied.

THE INITIAL IMPETUS.

In his presidential address Mr Ryrie Orr dealt with the possibilities of what might be done for young people by the libraries. He said they spent considerable sums on the education of children up to 14 and then destroyed half the effect of that colossal expenditure by bringing it as far as nine-tenths of the pupils were concerned to an abrupt conclusion. Much might be done by public libraries in affording facilities for study for those who were able to avail themselves of it. The majority of men must always get the initial impetus from education. But the majority of men and women were never given that effective start. They learned the three R's at the elementary school, and many of them had only that and nothing more in which to face the remote, complex, and constantly changing forces which affected their daily lines. No other light was given them upon the world they might explore. In every three years there were more than a million children leaving school at 14 who were lost to educational influence. There was no more crying need in the country to-day than the further education of these children, and it was to them that the libraries opened their doors.

A HALF-DIGESTED EDUCATION.

There was a grave weakness in a system of schooling that threw a large percentage of their young people into a careless world immature in mind and body, a half-digested and tenuous education their only passport to the larger humanism literature might give them. The vital necessity of cultivating the reading habit was admitted on all hands but the attempts to deal with the problem so far had been weak, uncertain, and unco-ordinated. If the reading habit were properly inculcated in schools, not as an outlet for the enthusiasm of the teacher, but as a result of a carefully considered part of the school curriculum, the task of the librarian would be much more hopeful. The provision of well-stocked libraries in all elementary schools seemed to offer the most hopeful results. That involved two main lines of action, very obvious to librarians. The selection of the right sort of books and the other was active guidance gently prompting the potential reader, bringing out his initiative, and directing him to read not at a venture, but in full understanding and enjoyment, until he found his way in profit and pleasure for himself. Methods of teaching must be radically wrong that left the vast majority of pupils with little inclination, and with still less preparedness for enlightened reading—the principal means of making permanent and fruitful the results of education.

LOVERS OF BOOKS.

It is a safe deduction that no child who has at any time belonged to a children's room of one of their public libraries would be ever anything but a lover of books. The conclusion of the whole matter was that whether children had books and guidance available in public libraries or in their own schools every opportunity should be given to them to discover that the reading of books was the most entertaining and exciting of adventures that lay open to them. The thirst of the child for the magic entertainment afforded by the printed page was often as ardent as the older readers, and for any community to extend to the least of its inhabitants that blessed privilege meant merely a little earlier starting of the young along the path which lead to competent and intelligent citizenship. Might they not in that way add to the forces labelled educational by which the present generation influenced the mental development and the character of the next. (Applause.)

UNDYING ROMANCE.

Mr Ernest A. Savage, principal librarian, Edinburgh Public Libraries, submitted an interesting paper on "The Boy as Reader." He said romance in some of the forms familiar to boys was disappearing. Pioneers had little new ground to explore. To older people it would, seem that the boy of the future would live in a melancholy world. Fortunately romance never died. It was the attribute of youth, and changed with, the environment of youth. Youth created romance and went to meet adventure. So long as there were things to make and successes to be achieved young people would fly to make and to achieve. Boys, they were told, did not like books for grown-ups, and would not read them That was a generalisation which must not be accepted, because it was desirable that they should be allowed to come at books usually considered to be suitable only for men and women. No creatures were more independent in spirit than boys. That independence they must take into account when thinking about the difficult problem of guiding a boy in his reading. (Applause.)

The following office-bearers were elected :— Councillors (retire in 1929)—Mr James Craigie, Perth; Miss Jean Cuthbertson, Glasgow; Mr Andrew Paterson, Glasgow; and Dr A. H. Miller, Dundee. Hon. treasurer and hon. secretary, Mr W. Storrie Beveridge, Edinburgh; and Mr Edgar H. Parsons, Glasgow.

The delegates were later entertained to luncheon in the Station Hotel by the Town Council, and the business meeting, at which the Council's report was adopted, followed. By the courtesy of the Right Hon. the Earl of Moray the delegates were conducted through the gardens, library, and picture gallery of Kinfauns Castle.

In the frontispiece of his 'Poems, Chiefly in the Scottish Dialect', printed at Kilmarnock in 1786, Burns has placed an anonymous quatrain:

> 'The simple Bard, unbroke by rules of art,
> He pours the wild effusions of the heart:
> And, if inspired, 'tis Nature's pow'rs inspire;
> Hers all the melting thrill, and hers the kindling fire.'

Of course, nothing could have been further from the truth of Burns at this time, or any other. To present himself as the rustic poet, untutored in literature, lifted from the plough by the Muses was something of a deliberate stance. It was a good selling line for a beginner-published poet. A purported modesty about his writing, which he did not feel, was better at this stage than an honest statement of his own worth. He had spent his life learning to write. From the first catechism lessons given by his father, through the excellent grounding given by schoolmaster Murdoch, and the continued course of wide reading begun then, Burns could be seen to be anything but an ill-educated man. This did not prevent him in his Preface, calling his first poems 'trifles' and— 'not the production of the poet, who, with all the advantages of learned art, and perhaps amid the elegances and idlenesses of upper life, looks down for a rural theme, with an eye to Theocrates or Virgil.' This was obviously no ordinary ploughboy. He had been rhyming since he could write, and by the time he was twenty, he was an accomplished versifier, but ostensibly when he appears in the public character of author he does it 'with fear and trembling'. He calls himself 'an impertinent blockhead, obtruding his nonsense on the world', and yet this is the nonsense that has since gone round the world and made his memory immortal. From the start he was a deliberate tradesman-in-letters, a craftsman-writer, self-taught to be so by sedulously aping all the writing he

The Vision

Excerpt from

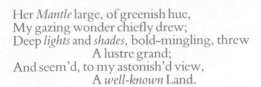

Green, slender, leaf–clad *Holly-boughs*
Were twisted, gracefu', round her brows,
I took her for some Scottish Muse,
   By that same token;
And come to stop those reckless vows,
   Would soon been broken.

A 'hare-brain'd, sentimental trace'
Was strongly marked in her face;
A wildly-witty, rustic grace
   Shone full upon her;
Her *eye*, ev'n turn'd on empty space,
   Beam'd keen with *Honor*.

Down flow'd her robe, a *tartan* sheen,
Till half a leg was scrimply seen;
And such a *leg*! my bonie Jean
   Could only peer it;
Sae straught, sae taper, tight and clean,
   Nan else came near it.

Her *Mantle* large, of greenish hue,
My gazing wonder chiefly drew;
Deep *lights* and *shades*, bold-mingling, threw
   A lustre grand;
And seem'd, to my astonish'd view,
   A *well-known* Land.

Here, rivers in the sea were lost;
There, mountains to the skies were tost:
Here, tumbling billows mark'd the coast,
   With surging foam;
There, distant shone, *Art's* lofty boast,
   The lordly dome.

Here, Doon pour'd down his far-fetch'd floods;
There, well-fed Irwine stately thuds:
Auld, hermit Aire staw thro' his woods,
   On to the shore;
And many a lesser torrent scuds,
   With seeming roar.

Low, in a sandy valley spread,
An ancient Borouh rear'd her head;
Still, as in *Scottish Story* read,
   She boasts a *Race*,
To ev'ry nobler virtue bred,
   And polish'd grace.

By stately tow'r or palace fair,
Or ruins pendent in the air,
Bold stems of Heroes, here and there,
   I could discern,
Some seem'd to muse, some seem'd to dare,
   With feature stern.

My heart did glowing trasport feel,
To see a Race heroic wheel,
And brandish round the deep-dy'd steel
   In sturdy blows;
While back-recoiling seem'd to reel
   Their Suthron foes.

admired. *As early as 1783 he began to try things out in his Commonplace Book. He knew that he could better himself more by implementing his pen than by pushing his plough. He went to any length to increase his knowledge and experience of people and manners. He attended dancing lessons, and walked into Ayr to take lessons in French. He even took up Latin, but as he said, "only when I was not in love. Consequently my Latin studies did not go forward!" But his bookishness continued, as Edinburgh bookseller, John Hill, confirmed. Burns was constantly ordering new writing as he saw it publicised or heard it discussed. So much so, that on his move from the farm at Ellisland to the town house at Dumfries, he had not sufficient room to contain the volumes he owned. He gave them to the City of Dumfries, to help institute its first library. And if doubts remain that Robert Burns was an educated prose stylist, let any one read his letters — surely among the finest prose instances of the 'belles lettres' ever to emerge from Scotland.*

The Glasgow Herald

147th YEAR—No. 256   FRIDAY, OCTOBER 25, 1929.   TWOPENCE

GLASGOW HER...

WALL STREET SLUMP

Huge Decline in American Share Values

CONDITIONS VERGING ON PANIC

THE POSITION IN BRITAIN

A great slump in stocks and shares occurred in the New York Stock Exchange yesterday. Early in the day the market, which has been steadily weakening of late, showed signs of rallying, but towards noon (about five o'clock British time) a tremendous decline developed, and conditions bordering on panic ensued. Prices underwent a huge decline and the volume of sales exceeded all previous records. It is estimated in New York that the depreciation in securities yesterday totalled £1,000,000,000.

Before the end markets showed a rallying tendency as a result of a reassuring statement by bankers.

The repercussions of the Wall Street collapse were felt in the Stock Exchanges in this country, dollar securities and others, such as Columbia Graphophone, which are influenced by America, undergoing very heavy falls. Intense excitement prevailed in the "Street" market in London, and business was carried on there in the rain until after 7 o'clock last night.

PRICE DEBACLE

WORST CRASH IN HISTORY OF EXCHANGE

ALL-DAY PANDEMONIUM

NEW YORK, Thursday, 9.55 p.m.
It is estimated that five billion dollars (£1,000,000,000) in market values were swept away in the worst crash in the history of the Stock Exchange to-day, eclipsing yesterday's ...h.

... 11,000,000 shares had frantically

EFFECT IN BRITAIN

EXCITED DEALINGS IN LONDON

CHIEF CAUSE OF FALL

With the news of Wednesday's heavy fall in New York stock prices before them dealers in London yesterday adopted a very cautious attitude so far as the considerable group of shares which are dealt in on both sides of the Atlantic were concerned. Prices ... opened ...

If money is recognised as the root of most evils, it was certainly at the seat of most of Burns' cares in the world. Its deprivation, or 'want of cash' as he called it, was for him at one and the same time, a continuing source of anxiety and a constant spur to effort. While he saw money as a man-made instrument of commerce, and knew its utility in the realms of usuria, he was well aware it had little to do with the essential quality of life.

> 'If happiness has not her seat,
> And centre in the breast,
> We may be wise or rich or great,
> But never can be blessed.'

Wae worth thy pow'r, thou cursed leaf!
Fell source of all my woe and grief!
For lake o' thee I've lost my lass;
For lake o' thee I scrimp my glass;
I see the children of Affliction
Unaided, thro' thy curst restriction;
I've seen th' Oppressor's cruel smile
Amid his hapless victim's spoil;
And for thy potence vainly wish'd
To crush the Villain in the dust:
For lake o' thee I leave this much–lov'd shore,
Never perhaps to greet old Scotland more!

He remembered enough of the Scotland of his own father's time to know that a peasant might survive on what he worked from the land, and did not depend for his life on the amount of coin in his pocket. It was this knowledge made him basically anti-capitalist, but with a traditional respect for the value of land—not seen as property, but as a base from which a man might live and propagate a family. He saw the family as the essential unit. All other relationships sprang from its basic core, spiralling out into society. If a man is sound in his family and secure in its ties, he can face the world squarely and confidently, knowing he is firmly rooted and safely based. However, with the gradual development even then, from the land-owning or lease-owning tenant farmer to the labourer, who was for hire, the need for ready money became more and more pressing. This is why the bank-note, or promissory statement, began to have a greater 'coinage'. It took the place of a previous barter tradition, and worldly success rapidly became a matter of amassing as much of this paper as one could, in order to buy not only life's luxuries, but its necessities. Burns knew little of luxuries, but was obsessed with the need to obtain the necessities. This had the effect of making them seem luxurious, and therefore appreciated and coveted. But:

> 'Nae pleasures nor treasures,
> Can keep us happy lang,
> The heart's ay the part ay
> That maks us right or wrang.'

Nothing so concentrates the mind as urgent necessity, and what is remarkable about his work is not its quality or genius, nor the extent of its range and output, but the fact that he wrote at all. One has to remember that most of his writing was done when he was penniless, unknown, uncertain of his ambition, resentful of his station, and for much of the time, cold, hungry, and unwell. He had to work all the hours of daylight in the fields, and could write only when they could afford a candle. Nevertheless, he was able to take up his goosefeather in a rat-infested garret, and as the extant manuscripts show, produce with hardly a blot, line after line of verse—some of it tedious, pretentious, but also poetry no money could buy.

The Glasgow Herald

162nd YEAR—No. 203. THURSDAY, AUGUST 24, 1944. POSTAGE TWOPENCE.

Scotland's Young Delinquents: "Children of the City"

FROM OUR OWN CORRESPONDENT

LONNDON, Wednesday.

It is unfortunate that "Children of the City"—screened at the Ministry of Information this afternoon—may never have a general release. Dealing with juvenile delinquency, this film is intended for the specialists handling cases of child crime, but the public should see it.

While the production is concerned with conditions in Scotland only, it mirrors a tragedy known in all industrialised countries; the plight of the town-bred urchin who seems to be doomed to trouble. His energy is forced down evil channels because he lives in a community that plans no place for children.

Made for the Scottish Education Department and the Scottish Home Department, this document is in the form of a narrative. Without sensationalism, the portraits of three young miscreants are drawn. Here is a Governmental essay of the better kind.

JUVENILE COURT

Alec, Duncan, and Robbie break into a shop. An escapade that starts as mischief is interrupted by the police, and the boys find themselves in court. Happily, it is the Juvenile Court which tries to combat the manufacture of criminals. Instead of being branded, the youthful burglars are cured by skilled treatment, and even the ringleader is on the way to reformation as the report closes.

But the final appeal is disturbing. Two-thirds of Scotland's population can be found in overcrowded industrial areas, where there are not always youth clubs and child guidance clinics for the Alecs, the Duncans, and the Robbies. Much good work has been done, yet much remains to do.

The setting of the film is an ingenious synthesis of Edinburgh, Glasgow, Aberdeen, and Dundee—the cities which provide too many ill-adjusted young people.

HORRORS OF CONGESTION

Ordinary people enact this sample drama—fictitious but typical—from the records of certain citizens under 17 years of age. Budge Cooper has directed his players cleverly, so that they appear to be natural, although they are never heard, the commentary speaking for them.

One or two simple scenes hint at the horrors of congestion. Not the least significant is a shot of an old, old man sitting on a squalid doorstep. He has been a child of the city in his time, and knows nothing better; for his grandsons there is every hope that life will be made both promising and good.

An unhurried effort, this puts its argument into 35 minutes without falling into the fault it condemns — overcrowding. The result is not nearly dull enough to be kept for specialised audiences.

In May, 1786, Burns penned his famous advice to his young friend, Andrew Aiken, son of Aiken, the lawyer in Ayr. Burns, himself, was only twenty-seven at the time, and hardly a man of the world. Apart from his brief time in Irvine, he had never gone further than a walking distance from Mauchline. It has been noted how untypically well-read and well-taught he was for one of his class, yet he was demonstrably inexperienced in the ways of society at large. However, he had originality and flair and was not beyond a show of local daring, as his dress and manner exemplified, but he had no firm base, as yet, from which to propound his views with any real authority. Nevertheless, in this epistle, he already evinces the warmth, humanity, wisdom, clear-sightedness and wit for which he was to be later renowned. Despite his age, the sentiments expressed are entirely validated in their relevance to the needs of the young. Shakespeare allows Polonius the famous advice to his son, Laertes, in 'Hamlet'. Burns' words to young Aiken showed that the Scottish poet shared the English bard's genius for encapsulating the universal in the particular and for giving to solemn matters a felicity and ease of expression. Beneath the flowing surface of the lines, there is an ocean-depth of good sense. The boy may be father to the man, and it must be stated that Burns' own father was also a remarkable man, to whom much of the credit for the Burns we know, must go. His mother may have given him those striking, dark eyes and love of song and story, but from his father's strict Calvinism and love of learning, especially in the written word, came the bed-rock upon which was built the enduring edifice that was the son's work in poetry and song. William Burnes knew that Robert was special. He told his wife, "Who lives, will know that boy . . ." Who knows what their talk must have been as they rested in the field or stared into the flames of the family hearth. Whatever it was, it gave the young Burns a unique insight and a keen observation, and it was this eye he cast

Epistle to a Young Friend

Excerpt from

I Lang hae thought, my youthfu' friend,
  A Something to have sent you,
Tho' it should serve nae other end
  Than just a kind memento;
But how the subject theme may gang,
  Let time and chance determine;
Perhaps it may turn out a Sang;
  Perhaps, turn out a Sermon.

Ye'll try the world soon my lad,
  And Andrew dear believe me,
Ye'll find mankind an unco squad,
  And muckle they may grieve ye:
For care and trouble set your thought,
  Ev'n when your end's attained;
And a' your views may come to nought,
  Where ev'ry nerve is strained.

I'll no say, men are villains a';
  The real, harden'd wicked,
Wha hae nae check but *human law*,
  Are to a few restricked:
But Och, mankind are unco weak,
  An' little to be trusted;
If *Self* the wavering balance shake,
  It's rarely right adjusted!

Ay free, aff han', your story tell,
  When wi' a bosom crony;
But still keep something to yoursel
  Ye scarcely tell to ony.
Conceal yoursel as weel's ye can
  Frae critical dissection;
But keek thro' ev'ry other man,
  Wi, sharpen'd sly inspection.

The *sacred lowe* o' weel plac'd love,
  Luxuriantly indulge it;
But never tempt th' *illicit rove*,
  Tho' naething should divulge it:
I wave the quantum o' the sin;
  The hazard of concealing;
But Och! it hardens a' *within*,
  And petrifies the feeling!

The *fear o' Hell's* a hangman's whip,
  To haud the wretch in order;
But where you feel your *Honor* grip,
  Let that ay be your border:
It's slightest touches, instant pause—
  Debar a' side-pretences;
And resolutely keep it's laws,
  Uncaring consequences.

The great Creator to revere,
  Must sure become the *Creature;*
But still the preaching cant forbear,
  And ev'n the rigid feature:
Yet ne'er with Wits prophane to range,
  Be complaisance extended;
An *atheist-laugh 's* a poor exchange
  For *Deity offended!*

When ranting round in Pleasure's ring,
  Religion may be blinded;
Or if she gie a *random-fling,*
  It may be little minded;
But when on Life we're tempest-driven,
  A Conscience but a canker—
A correspondence fix'd wi' Heav'n,
  Is sure a noble *anchor!*

Adieu, dear, amiable Youth!
  Your *heart* can ne'er be wanting!
May Prudence, Fortitude and Truth
  Erect your brow undaunting!
In *ploughman phrase* 'God send you speed,'
  Still daily to grow wiser;
And may ye better reck the *rede,*
  Than ever did th' *Adviser!*

on the world about him. He learned early that 'a man was a man for a' that',
and that the gift of life was something all men shared. In turn, his own sons
went out into the world, better prepared than he had been, thanks to a
conventional schooling obtained by trust fund and influential action by friends
and admirers of their father. Robert, his oldest son, retired from the Stamp
Office in London. James and William rose to be senior officers in the army. A
nice irony is that the descendants of the two illegitimate strains—from Bess
Paton in 1786 and Anna Park in 1791, produced a respectable progeny that
was proud to boast its Burns connection—although none was invited to the
Burns Festival in 1844 to join all the family then living in the half-century
celebrations. Burns' advice to his young friend must have worked. Andrew
Aiken became a successful merchant in Liverpool and died at St Petersburg.

The Glasgow Herald

169th YEAR—No. 198   MONDAY, AUGUST 20, 1951.   THREEPENCE

HIGHLAND INVASION OF EDINBURGH

Capital's Day of Kilts and Clansmen

FROM A SPECIAL CORRESPONDENT

The Glasgow woman, elbowing her way into one of the side streets, who grumbled, "There wisney a thoosand, ah coonted them," expressed the disappointment of the 500,000 who filled Edinburgh on Saturday from the Mound to the West End to see the massed parade of pipe bands and the public display of what would be the greatest congregation of the Scottish clans since 1822.

The disappointment was real though it arose not only from the failure of the police to control the crowd, and the consequent jostling of the pipers, but also from the spectators' own estimate of what they expected to see.

Like Locusts

They collected, determined to be impressed. They filled Princes Street from the shop windows and the garden railing to the tramlines; they spread like locusts on the grassy slope before the Assembly Hall; every balcony was crowded and every window; and the only man who was not totally hemmed in was one who was sitting on a chimney top half-way along the route. On street level vendors sold tartan favours and white heather, and a thin scattering of patient policemen did their best to control the invasion of a crowd which was good-natured but restless from three hours of waiting.

They expected a deafening volume of pipe music, and a procession that would stretch the length of Princes Street. But the parade—such of it as won through from the Mound—was past almost before they knew it had arrived, and it was only afterwards that people began to make the calculation of the number of ranks there really are in 1000 pipers marching 16 abreast. There were, in fact, something over 600 and, being unable to form up because of the press of the crowd, they marched eight abreast, led by Drum Major John Seton, D.C.M. There were two contingents, the second of which was the more thoroughly swamped. The first made a fine show of "Glendaruel Highlanders" and "Leaving Port Askaig"; the second, more overcome, found it difficult to strike up together, but by the time they reached the West End their drums were synchronised and they were bravely on the main of "The Barren Rocks of Aden."

delaying the simpler display of the occasion, which was the popular attraction, but one was ashamed openly to complain. One had too much sympathy for the sight of the gathering. They remained for four hours enclosed in canvas cubicles in the open space below the curtains of which one could sometimes see their feet tapping in time to the piping.

The other clansmen, adherents, and septmen had the freedom to pay tribute to such of their chiefs as countenanced the gathering, in the neighbouring field where in tented pavilions the heads of the clans and the presidents of clan societies held court.

Bannered Tents

There were 17 tents decorated with the banners of all the clans from the MacLeans to the Chattan confederacy. Notice boards identified the headquarters of Donalds, MacKinnons, Gordons, and Sinclairs; of Donnachaids, Campbells, Lamonts, and Mackays; of MacLeods, Rosses, and Munros; Camerons, MacNeils, MacNabs, Morrisons, MacPhersons, and Mackintoshes. The Hays' three cantons gules on a field argent announced the presence of the Countess of Erroll, Hereditary Lord High Constable of Scotland and chieftain of the gathering and games.

There was The Chisholm, alone among the chiefs with the definite article, which traditionally he shares only with the Devil and the Pope.

Coming out from the Campbell pavilion were two young clanswomen from overseas, whom one overheard saying, "Let's go now and look for enemies," and one noted the muttered comment of a passer-by —a MacDonald by his kilt—that such should not be hard to seek.

And as a background to this informal gathering there was the music of the pipes, not from the field, but nearer in the car-park and round the odd corners of the stand, where pipers, each man on his own, practised their grace-notes, or sucked the reeds of their chanters, or tuned their drones, or just played for the very love of it. Drummers beat little muffled tattoos, and a piper stood with his bonnet off facing a wall with his face in a corner, playing as if his heart would break.

75 Bands

There was a capricious wind and, to the spectators on the balconies at least, the arrival of the pipers had something of the qualities of the relief of Lucknow and "Jessie's Dream."

The first "Dinna ye hear them?" was answered by the siren of an ambulance, and the cause of a later hopeful listening turned out to be the whistle of a train. This impression of a thinness of sound which one does not look for in the bagpipes was happily dispelled some six hours later when, massed round a hollow square at Murrayfield, the 75 bands made such rousing noise as might have charmed the British Railway engines off the adjacent Glasgow line.

The problem of tartan identification was troublesome to native Scots, whose English and overseas colleagues and companions expected accurate and immediate answer to such difficult questions as why the City of Glasgow police wear the Royal Stewart and the Edinburgh City police the Prince Charles tartan, or the Shotts and Dykehead Colliery Band the Sinclair. Equally embarrassing as revelations of ignorance were the demands for spot identification of the tartans, of every hue from strawberry roan to off-white which were encountered among the spectators on the route and on the side streets and lanes leading to Princes Street. These could not be passed unnoticed, for there was an unmistakable feeling in the town of right of way for the kilt, expressed in a sturdy faintly bow-legged stride that suggested, with what foundation one would not dare to say, that the wearer had just come that morning off the hills and had not yet found his town legs.

A Day to Remember

There was, both in Edinburgh and at Murrayfield, a contagious sense of occasion an urgency such as could be heard in the voice of the man in a conservative lounge suit and a South-country accent, who held a child high so that he might see over the heads of the crowd, saying, "Look well, my boy. You will remember this day."

If he survived the cold and the driving rain of the afternoon the boy probably will, for there were impressive moments and such thrilling ones as came when George Clark tossed the caber three times running, and idled back after the competition was over to do it again for luck. There was entertainment on both sides of the grand stand. On the edge of the arena, one after the other the competitors for the world piping championship came on to play their march, strathspey, and reel.

The holding power of this particular skill is perhaps limited to the initiated. It was therefore without offence to tribal feeling that one heard an English neighbour, about 5.30, say, "It is fascinating. It's only that it seems so long."

This competition had the effect of

Impressive Ceremonial

Over the loudspeaker system the announcer recited all afternoon such messages as, "Will John MacNab, of Wellington, come round to the home-team entrance to the stand to meet his friend Angus MacLeod?"

The cold and the wet had thinned out the terraces when in the early evening the contests were over and the massed bands marched on to the field to hear the announcement of the world's championship and to receive their prizes from the chieftain. This last quarter of an hour was the best of the day. The massed pipers had all the panache which Princes Street denied them. They made the noise that was expected of them, and they relaxed their discipline to applaud their own victories with bonnets in the air.

And then the colour parties of the clans, who had been stationed round the perimeter of the field, marched through the bands, to halt in a crescent before the Countess of Erroll and to dip their flags and doff their bonnets while the bands played the salute to the chieftain.

DISCUSSION OF FUTURE

Lord Macpherson of Drumochter, chairman of the Council of Clan Societies, prophesied yesterday that another clan gathering may be held in two or three years' time. His personal view was that something should come out of the gathering to keep alive the wonderful spirit that was shown. The council will meet next month to decide future policy. Glasgow has been suggested as the scene of any future possible clan gathering.

INTERNATIONAL FILM FESTIVAL

"Man"

The fifth which is weeks from las Ed S

Burns paid only lip-service to the Highland tradition in the Scotland Story, as the stock Highland figures in his 'Jolly Beggars' make evident. Despite his strong Jacobite tendencies, he was the complete lowlander, in dress, in manner, in attitude and in how he regarded his fellow-Scots from the faraway north of the Highland line. He found their tartans as incomprehensible as their Gaelic, and the kilt was as incongrous to him as it still is to the Englishman! On his Highland tour he had little contact with the 'breekless hielanders', and in the one recorded meeting he had more than he bargained for! Riding one morning with a party of friends in Stirlingshire, a Highlander on horseback attempted to overtake them on a narrow road. A race resulted. Burns and the Highlander were neck and neck, when the latter put his pony across Burns' horse. Burns fell heavily, and the Highlander was thrown into the bushes, where he was left to 'pick the thorns out of his bare arse'. But Burns had broken his ankle! He was much more at ease as he moved away from the Highlands and Islands towards the Grampians and his father's homelands in the North-East. With people like Neil Gow, the fiddler in Aberdeenshire, his Burness cousins in Montrose, and the fisher-folk in Arbroath (none of whom wore the kilt), he felt much more at home. Burns dressed like the gentleman he would like to have been. He had necessary style and bravura. As a young man, he had worn a saffron plaid, and 'he had the only tied hair in the parish'. Besides, he had a natural dignity which never left him. He had little need to festoon himself in tartan to make an

My heart's in the Highlands, my heart is not here,
My heart's in the Highlands a chasing the deer;
Chasing the wild deer, and following the roe;
My heart's in the Highlands, wherever I go.—

Farewell to the Highlands, farewell to the North;
The birth-place of Valour, the country of Worth;
Wherever I wander, wherever I rove,
The hills of the Highlands for ever I love,—

Farewell to the mountains high cover'd with snow;
Farewell to the Straths and green vallies below:
Farewell to the forests and wild-hanging woods;
Farewell to the torrents and loud-pouring floods.—

My heart's in the Highlands, my heart is not here,
My heart's in the Highlands a chasing the deer;
Chasing the wild deer, and following the roe;
My heart's in the Highlands, wherever I go.—

impression, still less to wear a kilt to give himself colour. Yet what do we see today at every Burns Supper but kilts and sporrans and stockings and dirks and balmorals and glengarrys—all the paraphernalia of a Highland Games. None of this belongs to Burns or to his kind of Scotland, still less to the sober suiting of a lowland meal. He had worn the hodden grey before he donned the buff and blue. His only concession to exotic attire was his freemason's apron and regalia! Yes, there was an element of the dandy in Burns, as his preoccupation with cuffs and cravats during his Edinburgh time showed, but he was anything but a poseur, despite his prediliction for self-portraits and likenesses. There are no less than six accredited paintings of Burns by various artists, engravers and house-painters, yet none shows him in the tartan, and certainly not in a kilt. It had not been long since the tartan was proscribed, and the general attitude towards the Highlands from the lowland belt was just as indifferent. In their eyes, the Highlands and Islands had contributed little to the culture of mainland Scotland, its only significant contributions being whisky, the bagpipe and the tales of Ossian. Even the last was found to be a fraud. The bagpipe has been reluctantly assimilated, and the claims of whisky are still being assiduously studied!

THE GLASGOW HERALD

177th Year—No. 89   SATURDAY, MAY 9, 1959.   Threepence

House of Commons

LEGITIMACY BILL GIVEN THIRD READING

"Family" Clause Dropped

An unopposed third reading was given by the House of Commons yesterday to the Legitimacy Bill, the private member's measure of Mr John Parker (Dagenham—Lab.) which seeks to amend the 1926 Legitimacy Act by repealing the provision about an illegitimate child born when the father or mother is married to a third person.

Mr Parker, on the Report stage, withdrew a proposed new clause designed to legitimise a child born to a married woman and accepted by the husband as one of the family. The clause had met with opposition.

Mr David Renton, Under-Secretary of State, Home Office, said there were strong objections in principle against this new clause. It would be a short step from this to the legitimisation of all the children, whatever the circumstances, and marriage would lose much of its purpose.

Mr Philip Bell (East Bolton—Con.), also opposing the clause, said:—"The real trouble with family life now is that it is breaking down." Whether the child was legitimised or not a father or wife remained dis-honoured. No change in a name could change dishonour into honour.

Burns knew the importance of battles. But his weren't of the kind inspired by Blind Harry's Minstrelsy or the adventures of his great hero, William Wallace. No, the battle Burns gladly fought was with the flesh in the shape of Woman! He was introduced to the 'sect' at the Dalrymple dancing class, to which he stole despite his father's disapproval. Nonetheless, he persisted, and it was at a country dance he met his future wife, Jean. Significantly however, it was not until his father died that Burns was to 'know' a woman in the Biblical sense, and a child resulted—his 'dear-bought Bess'. He was twenty five and at the height of his masculinity, and Lizzie Paton was a young servant in the house. Burns refused to marry her, and the child, Elizabeth, was left with Mrs Burnes, to be brought up as one of her own. Mrs Burnes could never forgive her son for not marrying Lizzie, and in fact, from that time hardly spoke to him again. She spent her last years with her second son, Gilbert, in West Lothian, but must have known the fame that came to her first-born in her lifetime.

Scots, wha hae wi Wallace bled,
Scots, wham Bruce has aften led,
Welcome to your gory bed,—
    Or to victorie.—

Now's the day, and now's the hour;
See the front o' battle lour;
See approach proud Edward's power,
    Chains and Slaverie.—

Wha will be a traitor-knave?
Wha can fill a coward's grave?
Wha sae base as be a Slave?
    —Let him turn and flie:—

Wha for Scotland's king and law,
Freedom's sword will strongly draw,
Free-man stand, or Free-man fa',
    Let him follow me.—

By Oppression's woes and pains!
By your Sons in servile chains!
We will drain our dearest veins,
    But they *shall* be free!

Lay the proud Usurpers low!
Tyrants fall in every foe!
Liberty's in every blow!
    Let us Do—or Die!

national resentment of the shoddy way in which Scotland was sold in 1707. There was something more fundamental in his pysche, which insisted on his resisting any degree at all of Anglification—except, that is, in his letters, which were sparkling evidence of his admiration for an English prose style. Yet, he lived at a time when there was a general fashion for things English, especially in speech and manners. Edinburgh gentry queued for lessons in English speech given by Sheridan, and most of society followed James Beattie, a minor Scottish poet, in struggling to lose their native Scottish accents. Beattie insisted that poetry could only be poetry if it were written in English. Burns responded in a manner that is now a matter of public record and literary esteem— even his original volume was blatantly entitled: 'Poems Chiefly in the Scottish Dialect'. All his best poetical work was in his native Scots, especially the precise beauty of his song lyrics, so delicately matched to their haunting melodies. Although it must be admitted that in two hundred years, the world still does not know the words of 'Auld Lang Syne', yet stubbornly continues to sing it! Burns' Scottishness was half his genius, and almost single-handedly, he rescued a whole tradition of Scottish language in poesy that had come from Dunbar and the Makars, and pulled it forward beyond his own time, so that it might be taken up by Macdiarmid and the Makars of our own day. What is so extraordinary is that a young man in a small corner of a small country, should reach out unerringly beyond England, and span the world with his Scottishness.

SCOTLAND'S NEWSPAPER

CITY EDITION

GLASGOW HERALD

202nd year—No. 123   MONDAY, JUNE 18, 1984   Twenty Two Pence

...cess during a disabled bowlers match at Glasgow Green yesterday.

Picture JAMES CONNOR

Herald helps to save day

By ALLAN LAING

THE wedding went perfectly at St Peter's Church, Hyndland, Glasgow, at the weekend. But only because a succession of officials, up to one of Scotland's most senior registrars, worked behind the scenes to enable the couple who forgot to place their banns to get married.

Bride-to-be Linda Spalding, 21, of Clarence Drive, Hyndland, discovered the omission less than 24 hours before the ceremony was due to take place.

She was at home with her father and mother, Chris and Betty, checking that all the arrangements had been made.

Then the telephone rang and Linda spoke to Monsignor Gaetano Rossi, the priest at St Peter's. Reassured there were no last-minute hitches, he prepared to hang up and then, almost as an afterthought, said: "Now remember to bring the registration documents with you."

"What registration documents?" Linda asked, and dissolved into tears at the prospect of having to cancel the wedding.

The normally placid Spalding residence was in turmoil. They had invited 70 people to the church and another 70 to a reception in the Bellahouston Hotel. Many were already on their way, some from England and Denmark.

Mrs Spalding wept. Linda wept. Her bridesmaid wept. Even Mr George Melrose, the 26-year-old 'groom-to-be, shed a few tears in this flat in nearby Broomhill Drive.

Finally Mr Spalding telephoned the Glasgow Herald to ask what he could do.

It was 6 p.m. on Friday but we managed to contact a sheriff at his home. He explained there was one way of short-circuiting the wedding banns but he did not think it could be done at that time on a Friday night.

The next step was a call

Married at last: George and Linda Melrose

to an official of the sheriff clerk's department. He would have liked to have helped but unfortunately it was no longer within the courts' power to deal with such a predicament. However, he suggested a plea to the Registrar General in Edinburgh.

Mr J. S. Wheeler, the Deputy Registrar General for Scotland, was at home in the capital. He explained there was a procedure for emergency cases and, indeed, it required his approval.

However, the key man would be the local registrar in Glasgow. If he could be persuaded that everything was in order the wedding might yet go ahead.

Mr Joseph Gilligan, the answer to Linda Spalding's prayers, was having his evening meal in his Cumbernauld home when we finally contacted him.

The registrar telephoned the couple and instructed them to be at his Martha Street office at 9 p.m.

In a deserted city centre building Linda and George, their best man and chief bridesmaid went through the official procedures with Mr Gilligan.

At 11 p.m. on Friday, the precious papers clutched in her hand, Linda said: "If things had not worked out we would have been heartbroken. I couldn't have gone through with the church service, knowing that we would not have been married."

Waterfront

'In peace and content
My mind was bent,
And fool that I was,
—I married!'

'Be it known—to all whom it may concern— that Jean Armour is installed into all the rights and privileges, immunities, franchises and paraphernalia, that at present do, or at any time may, belong to the name, title and designation, WIFE of Robert Burns—Poet!' It is still a mystery how and where Robert Burns married Jean Armour. Was it in 1788 when he publicly owned her as wife and published the above to that effect? Certainly, he wrote to Mrs Dunlop in July of that year, "Yours of the 24th June is before me. I found it, as well as another valued friend—MY WIFE—waiting to welcome me to Ayrshire. I met both with the sincerest pleasure." Or was it the earlier 'marriage' when he wrote a paper to that effect, still binding according to Scottish common law? Or was he, in fact, married in Gavin Hamilton's sitting room? However and wherever it was, he was legally husband to Jean, and she, officially, Mrs Burns. They could now begin to found their family. Perhaps 'continue' is the better word, as Jean was already the mother of four when she wed. But she held herself already 'married' to Burns by virtue of that first paper of three years before, which was destroyed by her father when she gave birth to her first set of twins. Burns came back from his travels around Scotland to set

O My Luve's like a red, red rose,
   That's newly sprung in June;
O my Luve's like the melodie
   That's sweetly play'd in tune.—

As fair art thou, my bonie lass,
   So deep in luve am I,
And I will love thee still, my Dear,
   Till a' the seas gang dry.—

Till a' the seas gang dry my Dear,
   And the rocks melt wi' the sun:
I will love thee still, my Dear,
   While the sands o' life shall run.—

And fare thee weel, my only Luve!
   And fare thee weel, a while!
And I will come again, my Luve,
   Tho' it were ten thousand mile!

her up in lodgings with a bed, a sideboard and a table, thus making her his de facto wife. Following that egregious visit, he returned to Edinburgh, but left Jean pregnant again. She gave him another set of twins, both girls, but they died within weeks. However, she loved Burns, despite his proved weakness, and at heart he was as sincere in his love of her. It was only gradually he came to appreciate her qualities, and they were many. Not only was she a beauty, but she could sing like a bird and breed like a doe-rabbit, and, more than any, she understood her wayward, gifted husband. When Jean was pregnant with her third son, William, she heard that Anna Park had given Burns a son at the Globe. Her only comment was—'Oor Robin should hae had twa wives!' It must be remembered that when she had first met Burns at a penny-fee wedding in 1785, he was then in disgrace with the Kirk Session and his mother for Lizzie Paton's child. Then, when the Armours drove Jean and Burns apart, he fled into the arms of Mary Campbell. And, again, when their first 'marriage' was annulled by Daddy Auld, Burns dallied for a year with his 'Clarinda' in Edinburgh—at the same time seducing May Cameron and fathering another son by Jenny Clow! Burns was obviously no green husband on his marriage, nor a man to be trusted on his travels. But he did love his much-tried Jean, and when he died, she lived all his lifetime again, remembering that love, until she died on the 23rd March, 1834, aged 69.

POSTSCRIPT

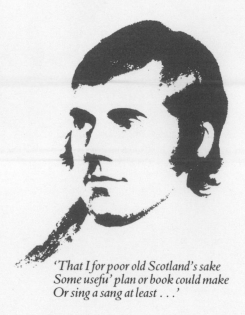

'That I for poor old Scotland's sake
Some usefu' plan or book could make
Or sing a sang at least . . .'

And so from Burns' time till our own day, we have seen how life has ebbed and flowed, and gone on its way. In the end, not much has changed. Essential man remains much as he was, and the problems and joys known to Burns are basically very much those that affect men and women through the ages. He knew well his own posterity, because he also knew humanity. If he had a good guess at his own posthumous fame, he had an educated intuition about the state of man in his time. We all grow old and in the process, know pleasure and pain as an inevitable part of life itself. Every life reduces itself to survival. Where once our ancestors scurried into a cave and made an image on a wall, so we now, all these thousands of years later, snuggle into a comfortable chair and read the words upon a page. We know the same need they knew — to be reassured, to be encouraged, to be stimulated, to be guided. All this we find in great literature and in great art of any kind. This is also what we find in Robert Burns.

We look back on two hundred years of his writing and aspects of his life. We also reflect on two centuries of ordinary life as seen in the columns of a newspaper. Between both, we should get an idea of how it has been for most of us for a lot of the time. What has been particularly recorded here has an overall general application. Out of the individuality and whimsicality of his genius and the variety and scale of the news items featured, the mix has attempted to present to the reader a broad picture of homo sapiens as he or she is.

Part of the joy in looking back is that sense of nostalgic re-living. But what is unique in reconsidering Burns and his comments is that he remains eternally young. Not because of his early death, but because he continues relevant and appropriate to us in our own day. Whatever our technological progress and supposed advances in material and environmental conditions, the finger that presses the button is still a human extension. It has feeling and sensitivity and a contact with the base and heart of things that is in all great art and in all the immortal utterances of the past. Burns' memory is only immortal, because he hasn't really died. He lives on in the best of the lines he wrote and in the hopes and aspirations of ordinary people who still live in the belief that the best of their days are coming.

Published by George Outram & Company Ltd., Albion Street, Glasgow
and Printed by Holmes McDougall Ltd., Glasgow & Edinburgh

Welcome To A Bastard Wean

Excerpt from

Welcome! My bonie, sweet, wee Dochter!
Tho' ye come here a wee unsought for;
And tho' your comin I hae fought for,
      Baith Kirk and Queir;
Yet by my faith, ye're no unwrought for,
      That I shall swear!

Wee image o' my bonie Betty,
As fatherly I kiss and daut thee,
As dear and near my heart I set thee,
      Wi' as gude will,
As a' the Priests had seen me get thee,
      That's out o' h———.—

Sweet fruit o' monie a merry dint,
My funny toil is no a' tint;
Tho' ye come to the warld asklent,
      Which fools may scoff at,
In my last plack your part's be in 't,
      The better half o't.—

Tho' I should be the waur bestead,
Thou's be as braw and bienly clad,
And thy young years as nicely bred,
      Wi' education,
As any brat o' Wedlock's bed,
      In a' thy station.—

[Lord grant that thou may ay inherit
Thy Mither's looks an' gracefu' merit;
An' thy poor, worthless Daddie's spirit,
      Without his failins!
'Twad please me mair to see thee heir it
      Than stocked mailins!]

For if thou be, what I wad hae thee,
And tak the counsel I shall gie thee,
I'll never rue my trouble wi' thee,
      The cost nor shame o't,
But be a loving Father to thee,
      And brag the name o't.—

Yet there is no mention of any intimacy between them. Burns never had any intention of marrying Lizzie Paton. They had come together sexually out of his grief and anxiety. She offered him comfort, and he honoured the issue of that physical union by accepting the child as his own and announcing his fatherhood to the world. This is the first instance of an ode to illegitimacy, firmly set down, as showing no shame in the resulting child. There could be no denying the poignancy of his honest pride in the fruits of love. For the record, Burns had three illegitimate children: the first, by Lizzie Paton, grew up to become Mrs Bishop, the second, a boy by Jenny Clow in Edinburgh, went to be a sailor at fourteen, and was lost at sea, and the third, another son by Anna Park at Dumfries, was taken in by Jean, and was brought up by her. Considering Burns' opportunities, this was a very small proportion of illegitimate children for the gentry of that period, who could renounce all responsibilities to the mother and child by paying ten pounds to the mother. But Burns was a natural gentleman, and embraced his natural children with all the love of a father. From his youth, Burns had tended to idealise women, and, from the beginning, each was held to be his presiding star. From the sixteen year old boy to the thirty seven year old man, his whole life was, in a sense, a procession of 'amours'. It is with awe that we note the number of love songs. Could it be that every one was a love affair? At any rate, the belles abounded, each drawing from Burns, a poem or a love song. When the final survivor of the Mauchline belles lay dying, she was asked if she remembered Poet Burns. The old lady smiled, and replied, "Brawly". Then she closed her eyes.

THE GLASGOW HERALD

189th Year — No. 51   MONDAY, MARCH 29, 1971   Four pence (4p)

Burns was at best an ambivalent Briton. It is certain he was pro-Scottish, almost to the point of xenophobia, and it is nearly as sure that he was anti-English. In Burns' eyes, at least as far as he refers to them in his works, they were little better than 'a parcel of rogues'. Not that he knew many Englishmen, although Captain Francis Grose, the antiquarian, was, and it is he must be thanked for 'Tam o' Shanter', since he asked Burns to illustrate a drawing of Alloway Kirk with a suitable poem. Earlier, Burns did touch a toe into England, by crossing the Tweed at Berwick, and ventured further on the same tour as far as Carlisle. But an unfortunate incident involving Burns' mare and the Mayor of Carlisle resulted in his leaving hurriedly after the first night—and prompting a verse which assured Carlisle that Burns' horse would still be a horse when said Englishman would be 'nae mair'! Whether this little contretemps was sufficiently weighty a matter to justify Burns' lifelong antipathy towards, or at least bias, against the English, one never knows. It seems to be something most Scots are born with—an uncomplicated, open and totally unreasonable dislike of their Southern neighbours. This may have its roots as far back as Flodden and certainly as recently as the mismanaged Jacobite rebellions. Burns always leaned towards the Stewarts and would share a